T0159104

Make It Intentional

Harness the Power of Positive Perspectives

BARBETTE SPITLER

BALBOA.
PRESS
A DIVISION OF HAY HOUSE

Client names and some details of their stories have been changed to protect their privacy.

Balboa Press books may be ordered through booksellers or by contacting:

Balboa Press
A Division of Hay House
1663 Liberty Drive
Bloomington, IN 47403
www.balboapress.com
1 (877) 407-4847

Because of the dynamic nature of the Internet, any web addresses or links contained in this book may have changed since publication and may no longer be valid. The views expressed in this work are solely those of the author and do not necessarily reflect the views of the publisher, and the publisher hereby disclaims any responsibility for them.

The author of this book does not dispense medical advice or prescribe the use of any technique as a form of treatment for physical, emotional, or medical problems without the advice of a physician, either directly or indirectly. The intent of the author is only to offer information of a general nature to help you in your quest for emotional and spiritual well-being. In the event you use any of the information in this book for yourself, which is your constitutional right, the author and the publisher assume no responsibility for your actions.

Any people depicted in stock imagery provided by Thinkstock are models, and such images are being used for illustrative purposes only. Certain stock imagery © Thinkstock.

Print information available on the last page.

ISBN: 978-1-5043-4599-6 (sc)
ISBN: 978-1-5043-4601-6 (hc)
ISBN: 978-1-5043-4600-9 (e)

Library of Congress Control Number: 2015920683

Balboa Press rev. date: 01/29/2016

Contents

Dedication vii

Special Thanks.. ix

Foreword.. xi

Introduction.. xiii

My Beginning xvii

Chapter 1:   Stinkin' Thinkin'
                Disempowered Thinking 1

Chapter 2:   Energy Follows Thought
                You create Your reality 13

Chapter 3:   Delete And Re-think It
                Recognize and Change That Stinkin' Thinkin' 30

Chapter 4:   What is Your Intention?
                Find Your Intention - Find Your Fuel 43

Chapter 5:   Make it Intentional
                Living Life With Purpose 51

Chapter 6:   A Purposeful Positive Perspective
                How to Find it and Keep it 65

Chapter 7:   The Ripple Effect
                It Starts with You 82

Chapter 8:   You have the Power
             Use it Wisely 98

Chapter 9:   Putting it all Together
             Practice, Practice, Practice 102

Final Notes 109
Appendix 114
Glossary of Barbette-ism's 117
About the Author 119

Dedication

To my children, Chad, Ryan, Britt, and Cody. You are my teachers and I am forever grateful for your patience, love and understanding while I learn.

To my husband, Damn-Near-Perfect. I am forever grateful for your insightful wisdom and incredible patience. Thank you for accepting me and loving me anyway. Because of you, I am whole.

Special Thanks

To my father for teaching me how to teach others what I've learned.

To Eldon Taylor whose books inspired me to explore the subconscious mind to better understand what we think and why.

To Wayne Dyer who inspired me to pay attention to my intention.

To Alice Flowers-Gay for the many hours she spent teaching me the difference between "writing like you speak and writing well."

To Laurie Hoffman who reminded me to "include your Barbette-isms" and encouraged me to write in my voice.

To my friends who supported me in this journey of life as well as the journey in writing this book.

To my clients for allowing me to share snippets of their stories.

To the many workshop participants who said, "You should write a book about this."

To all the Angel Medicine Members who recognize the value of this information and have embraced it.

To my husband for giving me space, time and encouragement to write, edit, and ponder.

To the Universe for conspiring with me to co-create this book and my life, which is exactly what I am intending it to be!

Foreword

You are about to undertake a wonderful journey that begins with the frustration so many know and experience every day, the idea that the universe is absolutely indifferent to their desires and ambitions. This is the notion that often leads to slogans like, "Life sucks and then you die." It is the idea that you are a limited being in a finite world handicapped in ways that hold the greatest treasures in life out of your reach. This is the world of frustration, resentment, anger, fear, disappointment, sadness and an unyielding sense of personal insignificance. In this world—most live a beleaguered life.

By contrast, imagine a world where your desire and deliberate intention is the force that shapes your experience. Just envision a world where you literally create your own future by learning to focus intention, like bringing the power of sunlight through a magnifying glass into that narrow beam of heat that ignites paper. Visualize this for a moment—what would you create? How would you change your world?

You now hold in your hands a guidebook that will lead you from the world of the disconcerted to the world of the co-creator, and what you do with it now is entirely up to you. Stop for a moment before going on and ask yourself this, "If I were presented with a map that would lead me from a place of pain to one of pleasure, what would I do with it?"

That is the choice before you. You will find exactly this in Barbette Spitler's inspirational book, "Make It Intentional." So the choice is yours, but my suggestion is simple: try it—you'll like it!

By Eldon Taylor, PhD
NY Times Bestselling Author of Choices and Illusions

Introduction

Every day we are gifted with the opportunity to reawaken our unconscious aspirations and to literally conceive and create anything and everything we desire. We have the ability to think, rethink, reason and wonder, pray and believe. We have the power to transform our unique and wondrous world with our very thoughts, actions, reactions and our intentions. And... We do! Every day is a new day. Every hour is a new opportunity. Every minute that we focus our thoughts we begin a journey that leads us to the destination of our choosing.

Whether you know it consciously or not and whether you believe it or not, you are creating your own life and your own reality - every moment of every day. Every thought you have, every feeling you feel, and every decision you make are all factors which make up your life. We have the ability to control our thoughts, our feelings, our actions, our reactions, and thus, we control our life. Contrary to some beliefs, we are not victims of our circumstances. We, in fact, actually create them. If you are not living with purposeful intent, then you are living as if in a virtual pinball machine, literally allowing yourself to be the little silver pinball. Without purposeful intention, you are being bounced from one place to another and probably feeling like you are just at the mercy of life itself. You are being affected by the thoughts, feeling, actions and reactions of others. They become the paddles that whack you around in the virtual pinball machine of life. If you are feeling as if the world is against you or you just can't get a break, then this book can be the catalyst that changes your life.

I've been a nurse for twenty-five years. I've worked with hundreds of people who felt victim to their life or the circumstances of their life. Patients, co-workers, friends and family have all used the same or similar type of verbiage. I've also worked with those who believe they are "just here" living their life day by day and waiting for something better to happen to or for them. I've seen people sit behind their illness as if it provides them safety. And on some level, for them it does. I've seen thousands of people who were hurt in their past and have turned that hurt into anger or some other type of angst. Their anger or angst is palpable. They are like a simmering teapot always ready to blow off steam. And because they are always simmering, they are easily brought to boiling and then they have to vent to release the pent up steam. They believe it is the fault of others for causing their need to vent. They believe the others made them feel this way or made them angry thereby causing the need to vent. For so many people, they believe there is nothing more or better available to them. They think and rethink about how difficult their life is and how nothing goes well for them. Maybe they wish it was better or maybe they have accepted this as their path. I call this "Stinkin' Thinkin'." Seldom do they realize *they* have the power to change it all! How? Simply by changing from their stinkin' thinkin'.

My experiences in nursing, health and life coaching, and teaching have helped me to learn and develop the ability to speak to people where they are. That means, at their current level of understanding. It comes easy to me. It has always been my desire to help people. It is also my desire to share what I learn with others. I desire to help everyone stop struggling and start living life more fully. It's easier than you think!

I have been reading books on attaining good health, preventing disease, promoting well-being, and self-help for as long as I can remember. I shared the books with friends. I often heard people tell how they read a book but didn't understand it or couldn't apply the concepts to themselves or their situations. When I realized I had the ability to share the overarching concepts of any of these books and in a manner which is easy to understand and apply, I began doing so at every opportunity. I love seeing someone's face light up when they grasp a new concept and see a way to use it for themselves or their family. My joy is in knowing they will cause a ripple effect of positivity that goes far beyond their expectations or understanding. For many years, people have suggested I write a book, too. I knew someday I would. And now is that time.

This book will help you change that stinkin' thinkin' leading to an intentional transformation. By changing our perspective and being empowered with understanding our intention, we can literally transform our life into what we want or hope it to be. The ripple effect of our transformation radiates outward, much like the ripple across a lake caused by dropping a stone into the center. That incredible, never ending, ripple effect has a beautiful impact on those in our immediate circle of friends, family and coworkers. However, the ripple effect doesn't stop there. It continues on through our circles and those with whom we interact daily or even once. Can you feel that? Can you imagine the global impact of intentional optimism and a purposeful positive perspective? It begins with just one of us choosing to make the transformation for our self.

Let today be the day you decide to take a look at where you are and where you want to be. Let today be the day you open yourself up to a new way of thinking, feeling, acting and responding. Let today be the day you make a powerful, purposeful, positive improvement in your life by setting your intention for what you desire and following through to make it all intentional!

"The more I study the universe,
the more I believe in a Higher Power."

-Albert Einstein

My Beginning

MANY YEARS AGO, I POKED fun at my life. I often said "You know Murphy's Law, right? Well, we call it "Spitler's Law". And it was true! If something could go wrong - it did. Whatever we wanted - we received the opposite. Whatever we planned – went terribly wrong. We laughed about it and made light of it. But, I had no idea how my comments and my musings about our rocky road actually worked toward making that reality continue and expand. I had no idea how my fearful thoughts often brought forth the very thing I was fearful could or would happen. My negative comments about the hand we were dealt often set the tone for what came next. Thinking I was just being smart, I would often make plans and decisions about future activities based on what could go wrong and then plan for it. I always had a "Plan B". I just knew what to expect and I felt so smart and so organized preparing for what I was sure was the inevitable. And more times than not, I was accurate. Plan B became the plan.

Our normal day to day happenings didn't seem out of the ordinary to us. We knew we weren't as lucky as our friends but we did alright. Occasionally, there were some great and wonderful events that occurred for us. I usually referred to them as miracles because, to me, they were miracles. Getting into nursing school was one of those miracles. (I will that explain later.) As wonderful as these events and opportunities would be, I continued to be ever so aware that it could all be taken away in the blink of an eye. In fact, I pretty much expected it. And as I stated earlier, I often planned for it.

Then one day, I attended a class in an energy medicine program that literally changed my life. I found myself devouring more and more information. I soon learned to connect how our energy follows our thoughts. I learned how there is an energetic connection to every emotion, every illness and every thing and every one around us. I learned how our thoughts become the very things in our life. I learned about energy vibration and intention, and how we attract to us what we think about most. I learned about the power we have within us to transform our lives. I read book after book and attended workshop after workshop. I very quickly realized I needed to make some proactive, intentional changes or our family life would continue to be filled with drama and trauma. I chose to "Make it Intentional".

I started a journey that has gone from a difficult expedition to an amazing adventure. And now my life's passion is to share what I've learned. It is my desire to help everyone bypass the terrible trek through the trauma and sail right on into the fantastic part of the voyage! In fact, it is my hope that everyone will hear this message and through their awareness of it, make purposeful changes that will become the steps that bring them closer to living the life they truly want for themselves.

I will tell you, though, it wasn't always easy. The self doubt and the negative thinking had been pervasive in my life for many years. I was the world's greatest skeptic. I had so many limiting beliefs and judgments about nearly everything. If I didn't know it and understand it, or see it myself, I not only doubted its existence, I *knew* it didn't exist. If it didn't make good sense to me, or it didn't feel right to me, then it just wasn't right. I held onto my beliefs and made them truths! When I couldn't understand something, I turned my attention to the things I knew to be truth. I thought I was being realistic. I tried to keep my sights on "reality". Not wishes and dreams but what I knew to be truth. Wow! Looking back I realize how short sighted my reality really was. I thought I knew what I knew. But my view of the world was limited by my life experiences, family teaching, religion, community, etc. My personal bubble was just one tiny little blip on the radar screen of the whole universe! But in my little world, it was all true and therefore, it was my truth.

When I finally decided to be open to making some changes I was alarmed. I discovered I had little or no ability to imagine beyond my truth or the truth as I knew it to be. I didn't know what I didn't know! I was embarrassed at how little I knew about life in general. I knew so little about the world as a whole. Frankly, I knew little more than what I learned in school. I didn't realize life outside my circle was so expansive and incredible and yet so frightening and somewhat unbelievable. My world as I knew it was comfortably uncomfortable. Beyond my comfort zone was more than just uncomfortable. It was embarrassing to discover how limited my beliefs and understandings actually were. Outside my comfort zone I felt ignorant and unsophisticated.

Yet, I practiced and practiced. Some days it was really quite painful. I tried to focus on the idea of "what else" or as Paul Harvey used to say, "The rest of the story". I actually became a "*more* seeker". I wanted to know more, explore more, see more, love more, and mostly, I wanted to understand more and BE *more*! I learned there are many who are seeking more. I know there are many who are not. It's been my experience that those who are not actively seeking the *more* out there are either unaware there is more (that was me) or are arrogantly standing in the place of thinking they already have all the understanding or awareness they need. I feel confident in stating they are either living in ignorant bliss or they are turning away from the many opportunities afforded them to discover there is more. Fear of the undiscovered is most often the culprit. Either way, they are simply missing out. I will venture a confident guess that Jesus, Gandhi, Albert Einstein, Mother Teresa, Benjamin Franklin, and any other deceased human of any other time period or at any education level would agree they wanted to learn more or BE *more*.

For those of us remaining on this Earth, we have a huge opportunity to discover there is more. The opportunities come every day.

I had some epic fails in this journey of growth and self development. Nevertheless, I remained determined. Sometimes, I took on the philosophy of "fake it till you make it". Why? Because I had grown weary of the old Spitler's Law. We had struggled far too long; we had enough drama and trauma. In some of my attempts, I had seen this positive thinking thing work with minimal effort but it was still hard to believe that I could fully change our current reality. Seriously, I thought? Yep, those old beliefs and fears kept nagging at me. The limiting beliefs were being stretched too far for comfort and the old proverbial "box" was looking like a good safe place again. Sometimes I wanted to jump right back in it. It always seemed safer and easier to go backward and resume the old way of thinking and living. However, I knew life there in that box. Even though I didn't like it, I knew my life inside the old limitations would be easier than stretching to new beliefs and understandings. Though I persevered and purposely worked to keep a positive perspective, it wasn't easy.

Friends and family are not always kind and supportive when changes are unfolding. People are often so comfortable in their discomfort they prefer you to be the same. Sometimes, as you grow, improve and blossom, others are fearful of what your new way of being means for them. The Ripple Effect of your improvements and changes affects everyone in your circles of family, friends and co-workers (Chapter 7).

I continued on the journey knowing there was something wonderful and nearly magical happening for me and for my family. I read books and attended more classes. I sought out workshops and began teaching what I was learning and experiencing, all the while, knowing there was more to learn. I felt as though I was fine-tuning every day. (I still feel this way.) We have raised our children to understand the concepts of how our thoughts become our reality. We strive to create beauty and love all around us. And we encourage everyone to become more aware and more conscious of how intention means everything. Yes, we still have moments of sadness or frustration - we are humans. But we remind each other to change the energy of it. Then we set our intention to change to something better. We change to a better thought or a better feeling. Then something better always finds its way to us. It's that easy. Understanding your true intention before an action or reaction means the difference between a desired or undesired outcome. It means having a better response which leads to better circumstances which makes us feel better and do better. The ripple effect goes on and on. It's true! And that's why this book was written for you!

Chapter 1
Stinkin' Thinkin'
Disempowered Thinking

I T SEEMS SO UNFAIR TO allow the children of our world to grow up without the basic understanding of how our thoughts become things. It's unethical! Understanding our intentions and the power of positive perspectives is every bit as important, perhaps more so, than reading and writing. Why? Because stinkin' thinkin' almost always starts in childhood. And it's preventable. It's so easy to teach children these concepts. Children want to be loved, lovable, and loving. They are also eager to share their love without conditions. Unfortunately, it's all too easy to squelch their gentle natures and turn their loving spirits to sadness or worse, anger. We inadvertently teach them our fears and our limiting beliefs. How many of your beliefs about life are the beliefs from your parents imprinted upon you? We restrict children's natural creativity and their natural ability for self-expression. Were you encouraged to sing and dance and draw freely when you were a child? We fail to recognize that their need for freedom, when restricted, often leads to self-conscious teens and limited adults.

Interestingly enough, beliefs are nothing more than thoughts we have thought often enough to believe they are true. It doesn't mean they are true. But we believe that they are. Someone tells us he or she had a horrible experience with a snake and we develop a belief that snakes are dreadful. Someone tells us the neighbor is creepy and we suddenly see his or her every move as sinister. Our religion tells us another religion is wrong so we believe those of another faith are misguided. Clever advertising slogans and marketing campaigns are built upon this premise. Advertisers want you to hear something often enough that you will believe it to be true!

Nearly every one of us can remember a situation where we were laughed at or felt out of place or worse, were bullied or made fun of by another student or a teacher. Seldom does the other person really intend to cause us hurt, long-term harm or sadness. No one purposely intends to teach us to devalue ourselves, right? Yet, the comments are forever etched within our subconscious. We never forget them. And if we receive other comments, thoughts or feelings which support the original comment, soon we believe it to be true. It becomes our truth.

Recently, I was reunited with a friend from grade school. We both attended an event and I recognized him. I study human behavior and can often be found watching the dynamics and interchanges between people or reading the energy of the group. I knew I would go over and reacquaint, but for a few moments I just watched him from a distance. I quickly noticed he was conflicted. He wanted to be outgoing and fun and participate in the group. Yet he sat quietly and withdrawn as if trying to be invisible. His shoulders were rounded slightly forward and he was slouched in the chair. He smiled and chuckled as he watched the animated group but he remained outside it. When I went over to chat with him, we caught up with each other and soon I discovered the reason for the inner conflict. He answered my gently probing questions with ease. He talked freely about his younger years and how his parents raised him. I learned that as a child, he was often told he "wouldn't amount to anything" and he often felt as if he had nothing to contribute or to share with others, at least nothing of value. He had little if any intrinsic value. Now in his early fifties, he realized he has made no real valuable contribution to the community. Nor had he any big success to show for his life. (I could argue for his contributions but for the sake of this discussion I will acknowledge that this was his awareness.) It was easy to see his inner conflict.

As a child, his subconscious mind had been programmed with the stinkin' thinkin' that he wasn't good enough, nor would he ever be good enough. He had heard it often. It was a consistent message delivered in a variety of different comments he heard from his parents. He felt strong emotion with it so it became his constant subconscious programming. On a conscious level he knew he could be fun and engaging. Yet, he had an inner recording reminding him he was not good enough. He felt he wouldn't be accepted by the group because of his inner knowing he wasn't good enough. No one around him knew of those thoughts. And since they were his subconscious thoughts he didn't have a full understanding of them either. Regardless, his inner dialogue continually led him to situations which supported his subconscious thoughts leading him to job losses and relationship failures. Now, I'm not at all suggesting his parents knew what they were doing. That's my point. Had his parents asked themselves, "What is my intention in saying these comments to my son?" they may have chosen different verbiage with very different results.

As a child, my family always made fun of my weight. Sometimes my brothers were mean and taunted me about eating sweets and where they would land on my already fat frame. I can remember far back into adolescence they called me names like "hippo-hips", "rhino-rump", and "barrel-butt". There was a lot of laughter at my expense. There was also the look of disgust that often came with the making fun, as if the teasing and poking fun were not enough. There were indications that I was disgusting to look at because I was so fat. Looking back at photographs from that time you can see I was far from being any of those titles. I was not skinny by any description. But I was not obese or fat either. However, I heard it often and it came with such shame and embarrassment I spent my teenage years internalizing the titles. I began sneaking food and eating it when no one could see me. I slipped away from others so no one would see how shameful I was. I ate anything and everything I wanted. I justified it by saying to myself, "I'm already fat and ugly; what's another cookie or candy bar?" I hid food in my dresser drawers and under my bed. When the mice invaded my Pecan Sandies, I was mortified! I was further humiliated because it became fuel for more poking fun at me. Then, I began to put on extra weight, too.

I carried that stinkin' thinkin' straight into adulthood. As a young adult, I continued to struggle with my weight. I would successfully lose weight and gain it back. Twice, I was over two hundred pounds on my five foot, seven and one-half-inch frame. However, once I learned how thoughts become things and how to rid myself of that stinkin' thinkin', I was able to change to healthier eating habits and was able to maintain a healthier weight and happier lifestyle. Can you imagine how much easier it would have been had I learned how to recognize and rectify the disempowering thoughts long ago? Again, it's not always easy. Internal dialogues from long ago are often deeply imprinted and a challenge to erase. But it can be done with awareness, intention and determination. Awareness is the critical first step.

What about you? What memories do you have of situations, events, or exchanges when you walked away with thoughts or feelings about being less than, not good enough, unloved, devalued or even unworthy or unacceptable? Can you remember when the initial thought was anchored into your subconscious? Are you able to see how subsequent events or life experiences fueled that belief or anchored it more fully?

Stinkin' Thinkin' is just a silly name used to describe a much more serious pattern of thinking. Here's a partial list of other words to describe this destructive way of thinking: pessimism, low self-esteem, negative self-talk, negative thinking, low self-confidence, cynical, defeated, worthless, dejected, distrustful, unhappy, depressed, bad attitude, hateful, disempowered, rejected, judgmental, condemn, disapproval, inept, unable, can't, shouldn't, contrary, adverse, unfavorable, naysayer, and detrimental. All those descriptions are destructive. Each one describes a harmful, hurtful, and toxic way of living and being.

Nothing good ever comes as a result of stinkin' thinkin'. You are either thinking "less than" for yourself or for another. Either will cause good situations to go bad or keep you from getting to a good situation. Interestingly enough, people who are struggling to reach their goals or for whom success seems to consistently evade them can trace back in time and find the source of the stinkin' thinkin'. There is always a root cause.

Most people are totally unaware they have some level of stinkin' thinkin' about themselves. They explain away their negative or disempowered thinking. It is far easier to blame someone else or another situation for the negative thoughts, feelings or fears.

Some people have an awareness of their own stinkin' thinkin'. They will tell me about all the work they do with positive thinking or positive affirmations. Clients will tell me about the books they've read, workshops they've attended, and lectures heard. Yet, they're confused how, in spite of their efforts, the blocks or barriers remain. They fail to see, feel or experience forward movement or attain consistent empowered thinking. Or, as soon as they remove one block, limiting belief or barrier, another one will sneak up to the surface making them feel like they're never getting ahead. One client exclaimed, "It's like there are hundreds of them waiting in single file to be heard!" It can be so overwhelming that many people will simply stop trying. They do not understand the source of the stinkin' thinkin' or how to change it.

In every book or workshop, there are messages, concepts and ideas that can facilitate our forward movement, personal growth and development. Understanding what to do with the concepts or how to integrate them into our daily practice is the key. Feeling supported while making the changes facilitates the transformation. How else can we know we are on the right track? How else can we feel the forward movement? How will we know what to do or where to turn when the momentum slows or another limiting belief surfaces?

Knowing the frustration of trying to incorporate the concepts learned from the experts into our daily lives, I started sharing the concepts in my workshops. Regardless of the workshop topic, I always include advanced concepts that often bring about great discussions. As we discuss the concepts, we each learn how to more easily integrate the philosophy of the concepts into our every day lives. And that's the purpose of introducing the concepts in the workshops and in this book. What good are the ideas, suggestions, or concepts written about in books or heard in lectures if there is no easy way to integrate them into our daily living? What help is the self-help book if its application into current lifestyle seems out of reach or too difficult to apply? Too often I've heard workshop participants express their frustration at having read the books and still feel like they have no understanding of how to put them in motion. Worse yet, those who are attempting to work the concepts into their everyday activities only to find they are experiencing backward movement or stasis - meaning no movement in any direction.

Our subconscious mind is absolutely amazing. Every single thing we have ever seen, heard, felt, thought, or experienced is permanently embedded in our subconscious memory. We cannot forget anything even if we try. That is why lying is so easy to detect. Because the truth is always within our subconscious memory and cannot be erased. We may have trouble accessing the memory of particular events, but they are always there. This fabulous feature of our fantastic brain is also the same feature that can cause us some frustration later in life. What I mean is that every negative or hurtful event from your childhood sits right beside the positive or helpful ones. Every comment the local bully said about you is etched in your subconscious. Every time someone told you how you couldn't possibly be good enough, fast enough or smart enough, your brain permanently etched it in your subconscious.

The brain makes no consideration for sarcasm. The words heard are the words imprinted. The brain does not decipher the sender's intention. The brain records the words and our feelings about those words. If the comments are delivered with a sick sense of humor, we not only record the words but we also imprint how they made us feel. The combination of the words and the emotions they elicit have the greatest impact on our subconscious thinking.

This begins the subconscious thinking patterning process. They can be pleasant and positive, neutral or negative messages and experiences. They can lead us to pleasant and positive thinking or they can lead to stinkin' thinkin'. Most of us have some of both. The patterning begins in childhood. It is the pattern most reinforced with repeated imprinting that becomes the inner guidance system. When those feelings or emotions are triggered later, the subconscious brain begins its internal dialogue of the historical event and quickly we are deep in the emotion of it again.

Here is an example of this subconscious patterning process. A child's peers laugh at him or her for being overweight. The child's parents tell him or her "you are too fat". Hearing new comments reinforces the message. The feeling of humiliation when laughed at becomes associated with the message. The pattern is initiated and when reinforced expands. Soon, the child's stinkin' thinkin' associates unrelated messages into the pattern. They see a commercial for a weight loss product and add that to the pattern. They try on a new pair of jeans that don't fit well and add that to the pattern. They walk between two desks at school, bump into one of them and add that to the pattern. The commercial was not created for them. The jeans were cut for a different body shape. The desks were situated too close. Each scenario is clearly unrelated but the subconscious mind records everything and files it away. Stinkin' thinkin' allows the subconscious mind to file the unrelated events into a negative pattern already in place. It's a complicated process. However, it is easy to repair, heal and reconstruct new patterns with positive perspectives.

For many people, the memories of those negative events are stronger and easier to access in our subconscious than the more positive memories. Dr. Phil once described this phenomenon by saying, "It takes a thousand atta-boys to counter one criticism". This is especially important to consider when parenting or working with children of any age. We are literally programming their subconscious mind with every comment, conversation and interaction. We have the ability to profoundly affect their future with goodness and positive perspectives or we can cause a great deal of harm resulting in hurt and anger which may take years to heal. Or they may struggle through adulthood and never find resolution to the internal dialogue of stinkin' thinkin'.

Several years ago I was at a child care center preparing to teach a workshop for the evening. It was closing time for the center and there was a lot of activity going on as teachers were closing down classrooms, children were preparing to go home and parents were in and out talking with the teachers and picking up their children. Amongst the frenzy of activity I happened to notice a young boy about the age of four. He was absolutely adorable and had a delightfully playful energy about him. I squatted down to eye level with him and said, "Well, my goodness! Aren't you just the cutest young man!" One of the staff members overheard me talking with the boy. She came over to correct me. She informed me he was not at all adorable he was "Chuckie". I gave her the quizzical look indicating I had no idea who "Chuckie" was. She explained that Chuckie was a character in a horror movie. She added, "This boy is evil itself".

I was so stunned by her comment I nearly stumbled while I tried to stand up. I was horrified. I was trying to counter her comments by looking him square in the eye and telling him he was a wonderful young man and how happy I was to meet him. I was trying to get her to stop talking while still trying to counter her verbiage. I saw the person who coordinated the evening event and waved her over. I asked the little boy to go play with the blocks over in the corner of the room. I did not want him to hear the conversation we were about to have.

As I spoke with the coordinator, the center director and two teachers also walked over to our little group. They each commented how he was a troubled child. They said he was always difficult and didn't listen to their direction. They informed me that it was common for them to tell him he is the worst child in the center. To top it off, they said the mother and the aunt also tell him how bad he is. Still stunned, I shared with them the gravity of the situation. I shared how the subconscious mind works and how each comment is being recorded in his mind. Then I shared how they can change their behavior for his betterment and make a huge, improved impact on his future. We talked about imprinting positive messages with a hug or a high-five so it will imprint with the emotion he feels as they give him the messages. One of the teachers asked if this would make a difference in how he acted in class. I replied, "If he feels better about himself he will be happier. If he is happier he will be less angry and feel less need to be aggressive. If he is less aggressive and disruptive, the energy of the whole class improves as does his experience at home. The ripple effect continues on from there!"

When we tell a child he is evil, terrible or anything of similar nature to being "less than", we are also telling the child we expect nothing better of them. We are programming their subconscious brain with stinkin' thinkin' that either must be rectified quickly or they will most likely fulfill the patterning we have laid out for them. It is a rare child that can escape that level of negative programming and become wonderfully successful. I am not saying he will become evil itself. I am saying he will most likely have a difficult time overcoming the subconscious programming. A parent using mindful methods to teach their child better behavior does not resort to calling them names, telling them they are not good enough, make fun of or laugh at them. Parents consciously wanting to make the best subconscious patterning for their children will imprint patterns of positive perspectives knowing those patterns will have the best outcome.

When I meet a child who is already angry and acting out, I wonder what events or patterns have occurred thus far to lead the child down the path of anger, hurt, or angst. It could be a difficult or very sad situation but it can be positively impacted with new messages and new patterns of positive perspectives. Most likely, the situation could have been avoided with the awareness of how our intention means everything. We cannot change the events of the past but we can put new, positive patterns in place and change the trajectory of their future. What a blessing!

Consider the true story for which the movie, "The Blind Side" was created. It's the story of Michael Oher, a homeless and traumatized boy who became an All-American football player and first round NFL draft pick with the help of a caring woman and her family. His negative programming was such that he struggled to find value in his life. He knew he wasn't smart. He knew he wouldn't amount to much of anything. He knew no one wanted him. Understanding the intrinsic value of every human, the Tuohy family accepted him just as he was. They showed him how he could overcome obstacles and be whatever he whole heartedly wanted to be.

They loved and supported him and encouraged him. They filled his head with empowering thoughts and cheered him as he progressed. They gave him enough atta-boys to overcome the stinkin' thinkin' he received in his younger years. Those situations make for great movies. It rarely happens in real life. But it can! Simply by harnessing the power of positive perspective we can easily recreate ourselves and help others as well.

I recently overheard a mother talking to her very young children. She was watching a Hollywood awards show on television and was telling her children it is "Never good to be rich or famous and it is doubly worse to be both rich and famous". She was quite concerned that her children could ever be like some of the celebrities we hear about in entertainment news. She said she wants them to be healthy and happy and be compassionate to others. She wants them to be thoughtful and kind and have a career where they make a difference in the world. Her belief is that rich and famous people are selfish and thoughtless and care only about themselves and how to further their financial wealth and their own career. Her beliefs and fears are being inadvertently programmed into her children's subconscious mind.

The imprinting of her fears and beliefs can become disempowering for her children later in life. It may be in direct conflict with their true life purpose. For example, it is possible one of her children may be destined to become a designer of world class energy efficient vehicles. This may mean great wealth and worldwide fame. The subconscious messages imprinted as a child could cause conflict for the adult designer. He or she could become subconsciously fearful of the wealth and fame and become a recluse. They could self-sabotage leading to a failed career or bankruptcy. Worse yet, they could give up before he or she is successful and never fulfill their life purpose.

I suggested, rather than telling the children what not to be, it would be wiser and more efficient to teach and encourage the children by sharing what you hope and desire for them. At the end of our discussion, she was smiling as she practiced re-framing her comments. She turned to them and said, "You are very smart. You can do great things in your life. Always be kind and thoughtful of others and always think how you can make the world a better place". Now, that's making it intentional!

Chapter 2
Energy Follows Thought
You create Your reality

IT'S TRUE YOU KNOW… YOUR energy follows your thoughts. What you focus on, worry about, ruminate over, and ponder take your energy in the direction of what you're thinking. Whether you intend it or not, what you think about is where your energy flows. Explained in more scientific terms, the vibration of your thoughts influences the vibration of your whole expanded energy field. Thus, your thoughts become your actions. Actions become habits and create the framework of your life. Literally, your thoughts will become the very essence of your life. Thoughts become the things of your reality.

Words are prayer. Ponder that concept. Pray is a verb. It means to plead, appeal, ask, or request. It can also mean pleading, begging, appealing, imploring. Prayer is a noun. It means a petition to God or an object of worship. It also means a spiritual communion like giving thanks, adoration or in confession. Many people believe only prayers can be answered and they are answered only by God. They may also believe true prayer is a special request sent purposefully to the heavens in hopes it will be granted. Many believe prayer must be done in specific ways or in specific places and said in specific or special ways. I am going to offer a different perspective.

The entire universe hears our prayers (requests, pleading or begging) and responds accordingly. Meaning, as we think our thoughts they become virtual instructions to the universe. And, it is the entire universe that responds to our prayers (aka instructions). It is the concept of the Law of Attraction at its most basic level. Yes, you can sit in lotus position, hum OMMMM, and send special requests to the heavens. Or you can, in a fit of anger, shout out how unfair your life is and sink into the woe of despair. Either way, you are thinking about it and you will get more of what you are thinking about. The more you focus on something the more of that something you will experience.

Most of us do not realize we have the power to improve our circumstances by changing those thoughts, prayers, and requests to the universe. Some people will believe that their present circumstance is just their lot in life. However, it is what we think about and focus on that we draw to us. You see, in our anger, frustration or woe, our energy vibration is low and more low vibration energy will be attracted or drawn to us. It is really that simple. It is also that simple to change it.

A key element here is this; unspoken words are every bit as vibrationally strong as the spoken word. When we silently pray with just our thoughts, is the prayer less important? Are our prayers heard just as well if they are only silent thoughts? Spoken or unspoken, they are the same.

Another key element is this; it matters not where we are or how we are positioned when we are speaking to the heavens or the universe. Our instructions are the same whether we are in a temple or in a department store. They are heard the same whether we are kneeling in church or walking in the woods.

Think back in your past. Do you remember a comment you made how some event would most certainly turn negative? Although you really wanted a positive outcome, you were predicting that it would be bad or negative, right? You told yourself how you really wanted it to go one way but somehow you just expected it would go the other way. Do you remember the outcome? Did you call it correctly? Did you "just know" it? If you are an intuitive person, you might surmise you knew intuitively what the outcome would be. However, true Intuitives generally remain neutral and detached from the outcome. More likely, it was you who affected the outcome by focusing your energy on how it could or would turn negative.

Many years ago, my husband and I had what we referred to as "Spitler's Law". We teased that Murphy's Law, the pessimistic little statement indicating if anything can go wrong it will, had nothing on us! We joked how nothing we hoped for was ever realized and it was always the opposite that actually came to fruition. We simply had no idea what we are calling into manifestation for our family. But, let me tell you, it worked!

An extraordinary story of how well Spitler's Law worked for us is the story of our family vacation in the early ninety's. Everything went horribly wrong. We had planned a trip to Florida to see our oldest son graduate from boot camp in Orlando. It was March, so we thought it would be perfect timing for a beautiful and relaxing spring break. We also planned to attend the space shuttle launch at Port Canaveral and visit some friends in Sarasota. Remember, we knew Spitler's Law would be in effect at some level. We had no idea what was about to unfold.

My husband borrowed his parent's motor home and we loaded it up with everything we needed. However, shortly before we planned to leave Ohio, a terrible snow storm pounded the entire region from Ohio through Georgia. Interstate-75 was closed through Kentucky and Tennessee for several days. We delayed our departure because of it. When we finally got started, it was slow going because of the backed up traffic. When we stopped for the first night, it was late and very dark. The campground attendant told us the open spots were at the back. We found a spot and got situated. We leveled off the motor home and got ready for bed. We finally settled in and then the ground started vibrating. It felt like an earth quake. It was frightening. Then the train whistle blew. As Spitler's Law would have it, about twenty yards behind us was a very active rail road. All night long!

We had planned for spring weather. When we arrived in Orlando we found bitter cold instead. Remember, it was the early ninety's and weather forecasts and news communications were quite different back then. We walked for quite a distance to the outdoor ceremony. The wind was piercing and uncomfortable. The bleachers were covered so the radiant warmth of the sun was efficiently blocked. Though covered, the bleachers were open to the whipping winds and near freezing temperatures. It was cold! Thankfully, the graduation ceremony was as wonderful as anticipated and even through the biting cold, we were able to enjoy quality visit time with our son.

The next day we drove to Cape Canaveral to watch the launch of the Space Shuttle. While awaiting the blast off, we decided our eight year old twin boys would have a better view from the top of the motor home. It was sunny, no wind, and finally felt warm. They happily and quickly climbed up to the top. They were so excited. Not only would they see a fabulous blast off, but they got to climb up on the roof of the RV. The ladder on the back of it had always been a temptation but they knew it was strictly off limits. For the boys, this adventure had just reached fantastic!

After they got settled, we tuned in the transistor radio and they were set for the launch. We listened from the vehicle radio. We waited patiently for more news of the astronauts' activities. There were hundreds of other people all around us. It was fun and exciting. Shortly before the countdown began, we heard a loud crunch. One of the boys had changed position. In doing so, he put his hand down on top of the plastic vent cover. It broke into several pieces and left an unexpected skylight in the top of the RV. OH NO! But there was no time to fuss. The radio was broadcasting that the count down had begun.

As the anticipation raised so did the expectations of how this blast off would look. The boys had been fabricating all sorts of fabulous visions. The final countdown began. Ten ... nine ... eight ... seven .... we could see the billowing smoke... six... five ... four.... then.... silence .... and then.... holding our collective breath.... nothing! Not today! The launch was scrubbed! Everyone was disappointed. We had been there for over two hours. As I shook my head in disbelief, I said to my husband, "We should have known. After all, we know how Spitler's Law works." We should have warned NASA we were planning to attend so they could have saved all that money, time and effort and rescheduled their launch.

The next day we traveled further south to Sarasota. Our plan was to play on the beach and spend a couple days in the warmth of the Florida sun. We prayed every day for no rain since there was a hole in the roof of the motor home. Sarasota was nice. We had friends to visit and sights to see. We enjoyed being at the beach basking in the radiant warmth of the sun and listening to the crashing waves. We love the ocean and the experience of being at the waters edge. Building sand castles and looking for sea shells captivated us for hours.

We began our trek home on a Friday afternoon. We crossed the new Sunshine Skyway Bridge. It was such a beautiful sight to see and to behold the view from the top of it was breathtaking. I had been looking forward to seeing the new bridge. I had been on the original Sunshine Skyway Bridge several times before it was hit and partially collapsed. I had heard so much about the building of the new bridge I wanted to see it from every angle. But it was late afternoon and the rush hour traffic was heavy. We decided not to stop at the rest area or the fishing pier. I told the boys everything I knew about the original bridge and incident that caused the collapse. We could see parts of the old bridge still standing. We were so intrigued that we didn't mind the heavy traffic. We were engaged in the discussion and we were enjoying the views and each other.

After we crossed the bridge the traffic suddenly stopped. My husband hit the brakes, we stopped, and we immediately felt a powerful thud. We thought we must have been rear-ended. The motor home was actually leaning awkwardly to the left. As my husband looked out his driver's side mirror, he was completely aghast and blurted out, "What in the world…?" I stood up and looked out the side windows. I couldn't believe what I was seeing. There were two entire wheels literally traveling about twenty mph, weaving in and out between the stopped vehicles. The wheels rolled past us, uncontrolled, and surprisingly avoided hitting anything. They rolled off the right side of the roadway and into the grass and came to a stop against the fence.

We still thought there must have been an accident. We had pulled off to the right side as best we could. Although the back end of the motor home wasn't willing to move much, we were able to get the majority of it onto the shoulder of the road. My husband stepped out to investigate. I tried to relax. We were safe, right? Traffic was moving very slowly. The twins were happy and playing. I pondered how those wheels had danced around every vehicle without hitting any of them. I felt bad for the owner of those wheels though. I wondered what happened to send their wheels careening down the highway. I was still pondering when my husband returned with a strange look on his face. I was not prepared for the news.

There was no car accident. We were not rear-ended. Thankfully, no others cars were involved. However, both wheels belonged on the left rear axle of the motor home. Yep! Somehow, they had sheared off the lug nuts and went touring on their own, leaving us behind. Can you imagine? It's absurd! Yet, I closed my eyes, shook my head with a sigh and realized it was the epitome of Spitler's Law in peak perfection.

We had AAA automotive service; we did not have cell phones. A police officer eventually showed up and radioed for a tow truck. When the first tow truck arrived it was already 7pm. His tow truck was way too small for a motor home and a family. It was after 10pm when the over-sized tow truck arrived. By this time, it was very late. We were exhausted. We learned there could be no repair work done on the motor home until Monday. I was beside myself. Spitler's Law was working overtime. The motor home needed to remain in the truck yard, but we were not allowed to remain in the motor home. The owner cited legal jargon but when I countered, he offered up the attack dogs and resident rodents. I caved. It was after midnight and we were out of cash and out of patience. It was not my favorite weekend.

Monday began the fiasco of the repairs. There was much more damage than just a couple wheels falling off. Imagine what it looked like under the motor home. The hub of the wheel and brake drum were 2 inches deep into the asphalt and the water tank was smashed to smithereens. After several days and hundreds of dollars we were not prepared to spend, we were again back on the road traveling north to Ohio. We stopped for the night and, thankfully, it was uneventful. However, the next day, as we were traveling through the mountains of Tennessee, we noticed that the engine wasn't running right. Soon, our max speed was about twenty-five miles per hour and we were struggling in those mountains. Was it the fuel pump? Was it the carburetor? Who knew? I didn't care! It was dark; I was frightened. I knew how things went for us - all bad. I pleaded that we just keep going. I was vetoed. It was Saturday night and we had to go in search of some place to spend the night. (I was sure I could hear the music from Deliverance off in the distance.) Did I mention it was dark and scary? We eventually found a State Park. The Ranger told us we were about 20 miles from the closest dealership but it wouldn't open till Monday. So, there we sat again. And then…. the rains came. I still shake my head. Yes, there was still an accidental skylight in the roof of the motor home.

Finally, Monday arrived and the motor home was repaired again. We arrived home the following day and did what we always did after such nonsense. We laughed it off. Actually, the entire story sounded too ridiculous to be true. It sounded like it should be made into a comedy movie. In our extended family, it's legendary! Spitler's Law was witnessed by many, but it didn't impact others like it did us. It was truly our energy following our negatively focused thoughts. The ripple effect rippled out to others though. Our in-laws quickly sold that motor home!

Here's another powerful example of how our energy follows thought. Later that summer, I had asked my husband to remove some scrub brush from the end of our driveway. It was blocking the view of the road making it difficult to see when pulling out onto the road. I had asked him repeatedly but he did not cut it down. If Spitler's Law was consistent, he simply would not comply. Why would he cut the brush like I wanted? Thus, I decided to tackle the job myself. He was gone that morning and I was sure I'd have it down, loaded onto the trailer and removed by the time he returned. It would be a big surprise for him. I had nearly finished cutting it and had it loaded on the trailer when he pulled into the driveway. He gave me a very disapproving look and said, "I would have gotten to it. But do you know that's Poison Ivy?" I argued it was way too big to be Poison Ivy because Poison Ivy only grows in little stems in the woods and was not the size of this huge brush. (My only experience with Poison Ivy had been just as I described. Therefore, it must be the only way it exists, right?) He was gentler and more tolerant than I and he recommended I go immediately and wash off the poison plant oil. I reminded him I had never been bothered by Poison Ivy in the past. Then I realized, with Spitler's Law, I'd probably get covered with it. I threw my hands up in frustration and I walked up to the house to wash.

I certainly got covered with it! My legs were blistered from socks to shorts. My arms were blistered from wrists to armpits. I was grateful I had shoes and gloves on. I was equally grateful I had showered quickly after the exposure and had washed the clothes and sneakers in hot water. My feet, hands, face and other areas were spared. My arms and legs, though, were 100% covered with a horrendous rash of blisters that lasted for three months! I can't tell you the number of times I had said things like, "It couldn't be a simple rash. OH NO! It had to be a Spitler-style rash!" or "Nothing easy for a Spitler". It was a long and very uncomfortable summer.

We worked hard. I usually worked two and sometimes three jobs. We struggled financially. We qualified for Food Stamps. We were on WIC (a federal program for low income women, infants and children who are at nutritional risk) when the twins were young. Our power was shut off twice. Both times we had come home from work on a Friday evening to find we had no power. The telltale red tag was on the meter. We lived on a farm with well water and farm animals. We needed power to run the pump for the water. The animals needed water and there was no secondary source. The power company was closed over the weekend and it was not considered an emergency to turn on the power for farm animals to get water. Get the picture?

I could go on telling stories of how our Spitler's Law lifestyle was everything we had created it to be. We unknowingly and unwittingly called it into action at every possible opportunity. We struggled at every turn. There were many times we felt the financial burden was more than we could handle. We always found a way. But it was difficult. And because it was embarrassing, we always tried to laugh it off and joke about it.

Truthfully, it was no laughing matter. More importantly, it was not at all necessary. Sunday mornings, while sitting in church, I would look at my children and smile with love and awe at their presence and the blessings they were to us. And I would pray for help! I wanted our lives to be successful. I hoped for all good things.

But good things never seemed to surface for us. If I had known how energy follows thought I would have changed those thoughts.

On a Thanksgiving Day in the late eighty's, I mentioned to my extended family that my lifelong desire had always been to be a nurse. I had been thinking about it again and I commented how maybe it was time I revisited that dream. Amid the comments of doubting family members I was defensive but I knew why they doubted. I had gone away to college after high school with the dream of becoming a nurse. Coming from a small town high school and going to a big city college was a bit of a shock. I struggled to fit in. I discovered it was not as easy to find new friends or feel good about myself in this new and strange environment. I thought the freshman classes were boring and they had nothing to do with nursing. The classrooms were bigger than the whole auditorium in my high school. Lastly, I had no idea how to handle the huge drinking parties and the campus lifestyle. College, for me, was a let down.

I went home after the first semester and returned to the local community college to take office administration classes. I felt like a failure. I relinquished my dream to be a nurse and went for something I thought would be easier. It's no wonder my family didn't jump with joy at my wish to revisit my dream of being a nurse. Additionally, in the several years that passed I had a very different life than a high school graduate. I was married and raising 4 children. The youngest were 3 yr old twins. I owned a busy cleaning service with several employees and I had earned many long-term clients. My family did not realize that their doubting my ability to be successful in this endeavor actually fueled my determination to succeed. Yes, I was like that in those days. Just try to tell me I couldn't do something and watch out! I was going to prove to you that I could.

My determination to be a nurse was in full force. It was where I focused my thoughts. Thus, there was also where my energy was focused. I wanted to be a nurse and I knew I would be a good one. The next day, Black Friday, I grabbed up the phone book (yes, we actually had a huge book with telephone numbers listed in alphabetical order by family name) and went to the blue pages. I found the phone number for the Dean of the Nursing Department at Sinclair Community College. I didn't think twice about it being a holiday weekend. I was determined! The Dean was not only at her desk, she actually answered my call. My eagerness was evident and she encouraged me by giving me a to-do list which I accomplished on Monday. I started the nursing program the first week in January. We were several weeks into the first quarter before I learned there was a two year waiting list to get into the nursing program. I had no idea. I was amazed, honored and elated that I had been able to by-pass that wait list.

Imagine how delighted I would have been to have learned right then these simple concepts of intention. It was demonstrated right in front of me. This single example of the power of intention was incredibly profound. It should have been enough to teach me the importance of setting intention and focusing my thoughts on positive perspectives. It should have been step one for understanding the basics of how our thoughts become our actions and our actions become our reality. Instead, it became one of several events which eventually awakened me to the concepts. I was slow to fully comprehend what was happening and I was slow to fully trust the process.

While in nursing school, I learned the standard nursing procedures, nursing care plans, nursing methodology, etc. And I loved every minute. I loved learning. I loved taking care of patients. I loved the homework. I loved working in the hospital and I loved teaching my patients and their families everything they wanted to know (and probably more than they wanted to know) about their illness and their care. Throughout the process of learning, I quickly realized there were many beliefs I held that had no validity. They were assumptions I had learned by trial and error or just by hearing statements as facts from someone else. For example, did you know the bones of the human body are just resting against other bones and only ligaments, tendons, muscles and skin keep them in place? Did you know those same bones can easily shift slightly out of place, causing pain, swelling and other agony? And did you know they can be easily shifted right back into place by a trained professional? Yes. That simple process, however, is frowned upon in most medical practices.

Chiropractic care is one of the easiest and healthiest modalities, yet it is still considered controversial in the United States. It's ridiculous! Yet, I, like so many others, believed only medical doctors knew best. I believed medications cured. I believed everything in current medical practice was the right way. I listened to medical professionals, whom I trusted, describe chiropractors as quacks. Their beliefs became my beliefs. Anything holistic or alternative was akin to snake oil of years ago and had no basis for consideration and couldn't possibly work. Or so I believed.

One of my early nursing instructors, Lois Lind, taught me as much, if not more, about life as she did about nursing. It was in her class we experimented with how the collective thoughts of the students could strengthen or weaken the test subject. It was fascinating! When we all held positive thoughts for the unaware test student, she was strong and resisted any muscle movement when tested. There was only silence in the room during this demonstration. When given the signal, we changed to negative thoughts toward the test subject and her ability to resist failed miserably. She was weakened by our thoughts. How could that be? Mrs. Lind showed us x-rays of how she used her own thoughts to change the arthritic condition of her hand from deformed to nearly normal. She showed us her x-rays! I was stunned. More importantly, I was panicked! Spitler's Law?? Oh Dear Lord, what have I done to my family!?!? Needless to say, changes began that moment! For the remainder of that quarter, I started on a journey toward the more positive side and I was amazed at every turn. I spent hours in awe. It was all so foreign to me so I watched, listened, asked dozens of questions, and I pondered… a lot…

I was delighted to discover that laughter helped patients heal better than sorrow and angst. Treating patients with respect, honor and humor helped them to cope with everything from their own physical pain to the emotional pain of losing limbs or being paralyzed. I learned the healing value of holding a hand, listening to a story, or just holding eye contact. I watched family members follow my lead in teasing with their loved one even when the situation was dire. And I watched the patients smile and relax. I discovered the horrors of medication side effects, not to mention medication errors. I began to notice how the patients of certain nurses seemed to progress better, heal quicker and have better outcomes than other nurses' patients. It didn't take me long to see that the happier and healthier the nurse, the happier and healthier his or her patients. Additionally, the happier and healthier the nurse, the better the physicians treated them and their patients. I noticed when the nurses and physicians had a better outlook for the patient; the patient had a better outlook and a better outcome. I noticed when a physician told the patient the prognosis was poor the patient's attitude would become instantly bleak. However, if the nurse provided a different outlook, some patients would respond positively and their prognoses would improve.

My studies, although observational only, proved to be great lessons for me. I became the nurse with that positive attitude and positive outlook and was thrilled when patients made significant progress towards healing. I remember going home after thirteen hours in the Intensive Care Unit feeling exhilarated. My thoughts every day were focused on making a positive impact and being a helpful, healing presence. I wanted to make a difference so I focused my thoughts on positive perspectives and made a difference. Surprisingly, it was that simple.

Then I learned how the purposeful power of positive people can upset the flow of negative naysayers who prefer the purposeful power of pessimism. When the two opposites come into the same space of existence, either a beautiful synchronicity occurs or one must acquiesce. Having no understanding of this phenomenon, I only knew it was becoming more difficult to remain happy and positive with several co-workers. I knew they didn't like me but I didn't know why. I helped them with their duties and was always available to help with their patients. Some co-workers were expressive and appreciative about working with me. They eventually shared with me how my happiness rubbed off on many yet rubbed some of the others the wrong way.

I allowed myself to get wrapped up in trying to win them over. I found myself trying to be a chameleon. I was trying to fit in with whoever was on shift with me. It didn't work well enough. I found myself looking ahead at the schedule to see with whom I'd be working. When I had a stretch of days with those negative naysayers or pessimistic pouters, I found myself feeling overwhelmed and depressed. Eventually I started getting physically ill. I had pneumonia five times while working in the ICU. I was trying to be something that was not natural for me. I was allowing myself to question my own value. Thus, I was inadvertently creating my own illness.

Why do I tell you all this? Because energy follows thought! When my thoughts were focused on happiness and joy and bringing those qualities to the patients I cared for and the people I worked with, I radiated. I was energized and was happy inside and out. When I discovered I made others uncomfortable, I tried to change for their comfort. Since it was upsetting to me, my thoughts were less than happy. I often thought, "Just how unhappy can you people be?" Thus, my energy waned and I lost focus of being the best I could be for my patients. I became frustrated and eventually began to dislike my job. After the five rounds of pneumonia, I was given a disciplinary action which meant I was unable to transfer out of the ICU for a full year. I met with the Human Resources department and asked for permission to transfer to the Emergency and Trauma

Center. My absences were well documented with x-ray proof of the pneumonia and I was confident it was due to the bacteria within the unit. They stood by their policy and, tail tucked and feeling quite defeated, I left that hospital. I was sad and depressed. I had hoped to be at that hospital for a very long career.

At the time, I was also a paramedic and a fire-fighter for a local volunteer fire department. (Did I mention earlier if someone thought I could not do something, especially because I am a girl, I would prove them wrong?) It was easy for me to move to the emergency department of another hospital. Again, I was the epitome of happy! I could barely keep both feet planted on the ground. Being in the ER was my dream nursing job. I knew most of the nurses and docs in this ER because we brought most of our ambulance patients to this hospital. I thought working there would be so much better than the ICU at that other hospital. Within the first ten days of my new position, one of the nurses I most admired made a comment that shook me to the core of my being. She said, "Hummm..... Well.... let's see how long it takes to knock that smile off her face!" I had overheard it. At first I was stunned. I was hurt. I felt myself going down that same black hole of questioning my self worth that I had experienced just months earlier in the ICU. Why??? What was wrong with me? What is it about me that makes people want to hurt me, knock me down, or make fun of me? I could feel the energy of despair coming over me again. And I didn't like it. Not one bit!

I mentioned earlier how a challenge against my abilities makes me determined to prove them wrong. Oh yes! This time, I vowed that NO ONE could or would remove the smile from my face. I was focused on keeping positive. I was able to find the bright side or positive perspective to nearly everything. I received numerous accolades on our customer service reports. As a paramedic in the field, I often received cards and letters at the firehouse from patients who wrote in to thank me for helping them. The positive reinforcement helped validate my intuition that people truly prefer happiness and joy rather than anger and angst. I worked with that nurse for several years. When I returned to the ER several years later she was genuinely pleased to see me. She told me she was pretty sure I was the only person she knew who made everyone feel good about themselves and who radiated happiness. Coming from her, those words were felt to the core of my being again. This time, they were received with grace and honor.

I will say it again… energy follows thought. Let me see how many ways I can say it. You are what you think. Your outside is a reflection of your inside. What you focus on expands. What you think about becomes your reality. Your reality is what you think it is. You get what you expect. Your actions and reactions are guided by your thoughts. You choose how you feel. You choose your actions and reactions. Your thoughts are a reflection of your feelings. What you expect you accept. Your words are instructions to the universe. Your thoughts and feelings guide your actions. Are you getting this? Look around you. Like what you see? If you do, then focus on what you like and you will see more and more of it. Not a fan of what you see around you? Dwell on it and you will get more of it, too. Too often we dwell on what we don't like and are surprised when we see more and more of it.

I recently read a series of FaceBook posts written by a friend who was experiencing a break up. She wrote post after post about how men are horrible, men have issues, she would be better off without men, etc. Over the next few weeks she had several dates. Every date was equally as horrible as the one before. Her thoughts were focused on horrible men. It's as if her instruction to the universe was all men she meets are to be horrible. So the entire universe collaborated to make sure her instructions were met. Her thoughts were coming from the hurt she experienced and she was acting on them. Thus, her energy was following her thoughts and she was attracting more and more of the same to her. One of her other friends wrote, "You need to be more positive". Hurray, I thought. Maybe that will get through to her. Her reply was, "I'm positive all men are selfish and stupid". Imagine what's next for her!

So now you must be asking yourself, what are we supposed to do? How can we possibly think only good thoughts? Is it possible? What if we think negative thoughts? Don't we all think negative thoughts at some point? How can we avoid something as destructive as Spitler's Law? What if we have a really bad day filled with negative thoughts? Then what? Do we literally have to police our every thought? Egads, that sounds like too much work! And more importantly, is it even possible? YES!! Not only is it possible. It's easier than you ever imagined.

Awareness is the key. You are already becoming aware of what you are thinking. You already have some idea if you are thinking thoughts that will bring you more of what you want or more of what you don't want. You have probably chuckled a few times while reading this and pondering about your own thoughts. Awareness of what we are thinking about is where we start. It's pretty much the way we start any new program or process, right? Awareness. Then we can engage with and adapt to the concept of change. Awareness begins the process of transformation.

Chapter 3
Delete And Re-think It
Recognize and Change That Stinkin' Thinkin'

THE TWO HIGHEST VIBRATIONAL WORDS on the planet are: I AM. The words that follow become either a hearty, robust announcement or the strongest command and compelling instruction to the universe. Using the words, **I am,** mean you are claiming the statement as your truth, whether it is or isn't. You claim it and it soon will become your truth. Stating, **I am,** is an effective and persuasive call to action. It is a calling to all energetic forces to comply with your wish. When it is accompanied with heartfelt emotion and belief, it becomes an authoritarian directive.

Ah, so you say it is not your *actual* desire you are shouting out to the universe? What? You mean you are being sarcastic, facetious, or you're just kidding? Yet, somehow God, his angelic realm and the entire universe are supposed to know what you really mean? Well, take a deep breath and brace yourself; it doesn't work that way. There is much truth in the old adage "Say what you mean and mean what you say". Truly, we must pay attention to our intention. Sarcasm is a human trait lost on the spiritual realm. Just to be clear, any statement said with sarcasm has a thread of truth hidden within the veil of humor. Sarcasm is a human way of trying to hide true feelings behind a thin layer of something that presents like humor. Sarcasm can be quite confusing for many people. Those on the spectrum of Autism are unable to hear the failed attempt at humor and instead hear the statements as they are said. The statements themselves often make no sense. Sarcasm isn't really humor at all. It is simply a way of sneering at, making fun of or making cutting remarks about something. It is not healthy, helpful or healing in any way. It's just another form of stinkin' thinkin' and we already know where that leads.

I literally cringe when I hear people announce their imperfection or weakness and claim it to be so. For example, "I am so fat". Or "It's hell getting old". Announce it. Claim it. And it will be yours. Why? Because you believe it to be so and you are either purposely or unwittingly, instructing the universe to make sure it happens to you or for you. At some level, whether it's intentional or not, you already believe it and have decided it must be your truth. Even in jest, the words thought or spoken are taken literally. Remember, I was the queen of cursing our family with Spitler's Law so I totally understand how this concept works. Because I was so good at it, I easily recognize it when I see it or hear it. And I am quick to offer a different perspective to the purveyor of such proclivity. (I genuinely enjoy playing with words.)

In the back of this book, you will find lists of disempowering statements or thoughts matched with more empowering statements. Since we all have them, those little rascals I call disempowering thoughts, we will do well for ourselves to be able to recognize them. The key to this concept is to identify them and then to quickly and efficiently change them. That's where "delete that" fits in to the process. My favorite is "delete, delete, delete". I say it often, and usually with gusto. Otherwise, you will continue the cycle of disempowered stinkin' thinkin' and continue to create a life of all the things you don't want rather than what you do want. There is another saying that deserves repeating here: "Be careful what you wish for, you just might get it."

Let's talk verbiage. I explained about sarcasm already. As I said earlier, it is important to say what you mean and to mean what you say. Silly as it sounds, it's true at such a deep and profound level we must examine it more fully. Teasing and playful banter can be fun for humans in general conversations or discussions. However, when we are giving directions or instructions, the teasing becomes useless extra words which take our attention away from the directions. The extra verbiage can confuse the listener and distract them from the right path. Therefore, when giving directions or instructions, being brief and concise is best. How can we be brief and concise most efficiently? By saying what we want, NOT what we don't want.

Here is a profound example from my own experience. In my past, I had experienced a series of head injuries. They ranged from sports injuries to misjudging heights of objects to a serious car accident and more. The head injury from the car accident resulted in vision, hearing and complex speech issues. My physician voiced his concern about too many concussions. He was concerned about how another serious head injury might seriously affect me. While attending an energy medicine workshop, I had shared my concern over so many head injuries. Later in the workshop we were discussing messages the universe gives us. I remember laughing as I shared with the class and the instructor, "I ask the universe to hit me over the head with messages because I just don't hear them and seldom see them". The instructor stared at me in disbelief. I was puzzled. Here she was staring at me with her jaw hanging open and I thought it was a cute little joke. She didn't giggle. In fact, she said "Ever consider why you get so many head injuries? NEVER say those words again!" I remarked how I was just teasing and didn't *really* want to be hit over the head. Her wise words were; "The universe responds to exactly what you say". Now it was my turn to stare in disbelief, jaw hanging open, as I immediately saw what I was manifesting for myself and my family. Wow. It was another life altering moment. It exposed another layer of how thoughts become our reality. I wish I had been introduced to this concept when I was much younger. My entire adulthood would have been so different. *Proactive* and *intentional* would have been my buzz words rather than *that never works for us* and *we always get the worst of...*

Have you ever noticed, when telling a child what not to do, they turn right around and DO IT!? We tell them, "Don't you hit your sister". The next moment, they hit their sister. We are left wondering if we are terrible parents or if our child is just obnoxiously defiant. What we know is this: children do not understand contractions. Contractions (don't, won't, couldn't, shouldn't) are strange words that have no picture associated with them. Think about it. It takes years to understand the concept of their usage in sentences and many cultures or other languages simply have no translation for them. Contractions are not easy for children to comprehend; children under six to eight years old (depending on development) really have no concept for them. We may tell a child, "Don't play in the street" and what they hear is, "blah.... play in the street". They look at us like we've gone crazy and then they head toward the street. Eventually they may learn by the non-verbal cues like tone of voice, the physical stance of the speaker or the look on his or her face, that the speaker means business. They may begin to associate fear of punishment with the statement holding the contraction. Eventually, they get the message but there is no true understanding of the meaning and no picture to associate with it.

It is much simpler and significantly more efficient to say what we want and what we expect instead. For example, "Play on the sidewalk because it is safer", or "Be gentle with your sister". When we focus on what we want, we get it. When we focus on what we do not want, we get it. Speaking to children about what we expect from them, they will respond accordingly. Telling children what we want them to do, they will focus on what we want them to do. Tell them what you don't want and they will do exactly what you don't want. It's really that simple!! It's so easy to work with children in the context of speaking clearly and concisely about what we want them to do. They are eager to reap the positivity we express when they comply with the request.

It's the same concept for setting our intention, speaking our truth, or requesting Divine Intervention. In addition to being clear and concise and saying what we truly mean, efficient calls to the universe are best when they are focused on what we want - never the contrary. As the universe hears and responds to our desires and instructions, there is very little or no wiggle room for slang terms, differences in usage by culture or subcultures, speaking in metaphors or statements like, "you know what I mean". When you say exactly what you mean there is no room for interpretation. The universe responds to all humans on the planet. Imagine the spiritual realm attempting to interpret the true meanings of all requests. Oh, the chaos! Moreover, as we humans have free will, the spiritual realm cannot choose for us. Otherwise, we would truly want for nothing as any messenger of the heavens would certainly want us to have all our wishes fulfilled and our desire for abundance met with joy and happiness. Right? Of course! They do want us to have all our wishes fulfilled. That is precisely why they respond so readily to our spoken wishes or our thoughts. See the irony? We have to pay attention to our intention. Be mindful of our thoughts and thinking patterns.

We must acknowledge, in American culture, words can have different and sometimes odd meanings. For example, fat means overweight. In slang, phat, which sounds the same as fat, means cool, or really hot. When a young lady looks in the mirror and says, "I'm so fat", the universe hears her command to keep her overweight and will politely comply with her request. If, however, she meant, "I'm so phat", do you suppose the universe will just know the difference? Verbiage is important in general conversations but even more so when asking for help, giving directions, or following instructions. I cannot emphasize this concept enough. Say what you mean, mean what you say, and be careful what you wish for. Words are prayer and prayers are universal instruction.

Prayer in relation to universal instruction is an interesting subject to explore further. Taking the word prayer at it's most literal; it is a spiritual communion or connection with a higher power. Whatever we want to call it: Prayer, Divine Intervention, spiritual guidance, universal commands, connecting to spirit, or prayer requests. In whatever form we do it: In a spiritual building, while in meditation, in the shower, on a distance run, in a fit of anger or even in the bathroom. Each way is a spiritual communion or connection with a higher power. Again, it matters not how you pray or where you pray. Your thinking becomes your prayer and those prayers get answered.

I have a friend who only considers prayer as something to be performed while in church. I know many people who commune with Spirit throughout the day for dozens of different reasons, and sometimes for only a moment at a time. Each of these is conscious conversation (prayer) and that's what works for them. Ponder for a moment what your process is for connecting to Spirit and asking for guidance or seeking assistance. Maybe now is a good time to stop reading this chapter and spend a few moments writing down your thoughts. What does prayer mean to you and how do you do it? Are you open to a different process? Do you pray for yourself?

Now, contemplate how all your thoughts are prayers, even when you are not purposefully praying or asking for guidance or assistance. Yes, it is the subconscious thoughts, the thoughts we have when we are absentmindedly going through our day, that need our attention. Subconscious thoughts are the most prevalent of our thinking. They are the short little comments we make about ourselves when we look in the mirror and hastily look away. They are the quick little judgments we make about another's clothes, shoes, hair, skin color, or accent. They are the brief glimpses of old memories that flash quickly in our minds and they are the thoughts and emotions that come with them. It is the beliefs we embraced as children that are also anchored deeply within our subconscious.

Old fears and fables are also found in the subconscious mind. They are old beliefs and repetitive thoughts that may not even match with our current way of conscious thinking. Those deeply held beliefs often find a foothold in our subconscious and we hold onto them. The subconscious thinking is where we find our most common, habitual, prevailing thinking about our self, our situation, our life, our history, our traumas and dramas. Because these thoughts are the most habitual, the subconscious always wins. Unless we learn how to change them, they limit us our entire life. The subconscious is also where we find our deepest emotions and the secret thoughts we keep hidden away. Or so we think we keep them hidden. They actually have become the framework of our current life.

Several years ago I was mesmerized by the show "Survivor". Early on, I found it to be a wonderful study on human behavior. The participants were stressed on many levels and more often than not, they lost their ability to maintain their composure and self control. During the second season, Australian Outback, one of the participants complained she was made to look worse than she was in person. Her name was Jerri and she claimed it was all the stress of being so tired and hungry that "you become something you aren't". I remember shaking my head, and saying out loud to the TV, "anyone can be anything until they are stressed and then their true nature is revealed." You see, we can consciously choose to be kind and considerate when we want or need to be. But if our true nature (our subconscious) is angry and self-centered, as soon as our confidence is shaken or our composure challenged, we are pressed and overstressed, or enough alcohol has been consumed, then our cover is blown and our inner being, our secret self is revealed.

This might be another good opportunity to spend a few moments writing about how you feel when overly tired or stressed. Are you exhausted but still smiling and a little silly? Or are you easily annoyed and quick to bark at someone? When stressed do you cry easily and find yourself wanting to crawl into the corner? Do you head to the cupboard and seek out sweets or salty snacks? Do you yell at everyone and tell them how stupid they seem? It may seem unimportant to do this simple exercise, but it helps us recognize what our subconscious thinking is focused on so we can change that stinkin' thinkin'. The quicker we recognize it and change it, the quicker we can make positive improvements and positively impact every aspect of our life.

Every day we are faced with negative people, negative behaviors, or our own negative thoughts about our self or others. It is virtually impossible to avoid all negativity, nor do we need to. We just need to recognize it when we see it, feel it, hear it, or think it. As soon as we recognize the stinkin' thinkin', (knowing those thoughts are our virtual instructions to the universe) we can quickly cancel, clear, or delete them and send out new, more valuable, higher quality instructions that more closely reflect what we truly desire. How? Much the same way as we erase pencil markings from paper, delete typed letters from the computer screen or even paint over graffiti. As soon as we notice the effect isn't what we want, we erase and start over. Or we back space and write again. Or we clear the canvas and begin anew. It's that simple. If you are a visual person, visualize the wording disappear and new verbiage replacing it. Or visualize the clean white board and rewrite your statement.

A lady in one of my workshops said she liked the idea of putting the whole thought in an imaginary balloon and releasing it to the heavens. She then visualized animated characters crafting her new statement with her and saw it painted on a huge white wall. A man in another workshop threw his cancelled statement into an imaginary fire off to his left. Then he repeated his new statement 3 times for added emphasis. My friend just waves her hand and says "cancel".

Then she reframes the statement out loud. Another friend says, "Cancel, clear, delete". Another uses both her hands like erasers and erases the statement. Do what works for you. Just do it!

In my workshops and with my clients, when someone uses self-defeating language, I simply say "delete that" or "delete, delete, delete" while adding a Pac-Man like gesture to show the gobbling up of the wording. It's become sort of my trademark gesture. So much so that when a friend on FaceBook had written a particularly self-defeating post, I commented on the thread, "delete that" and went on my merry way. Later, I realized what I had done and that she had not been to one of my workshops and perhaps wouldn't know what I meant by the remark. Sure enough, the entire post and accompanying thread were missing. I had not intended for her to literally delete the post, just the energy and intention behind it. I hurriedly sent her a private message to explain what I had thoughtlessly done and what I meant and how I hoped she wasn't upset. She said she understood and I was right; the post needed to be deleted. She also said she knew she needed help with deleting other self-defeating thoughts and replacing them with more positive ones. She was eager to embrace the concept.

This takes practice! We have approximately ninety thousand thoughts every day. It is estimated that eighty percent of those thoughts are negative. However, the more we practice this process of canceling or deleting thoughts focused on what we do NOT want and exchanging them for thoughts aligned with what we DO want, the easier the process becomes. And, the more natural it will be to think uplifting or positive thoughts more frequently. Even a twenty percent improvement would be significant. Imagine a whole world where eighty percent of thoughts would be positive and uplifting and only twenty percent would be negative. Now that would be some fabulous place to be! It's easier than you may think it is. However, I must share with you that this process is on-going. In my experience, it seems never ending.

I know the process and I know it well. Yet, I find myself deleting or canceling statements and thoughts every day. There are times I catch myself mid-sentence. Yeah for me! Other times I may be deep in an emotion of something I do not like nor want before I have the awareness to change my thoughts about it. The longer we sit in the emotion of something we do not like, the easier it is to stay there. The longer we stay there in that emotion, the more of the same will be drawn to us. It takes awareness of wanting something better and a concentrated effort to change our thoughts to something better to actually achieve the something better.

This concept is also worth sharing with others. When my friends and I are having lighthearted conversation, we may catch each other with self-defeating comments or judgments and we "delete" them (aloud) for each other. We giggle and move on. My husband and our adult children are very well aware of this concept and at times, in the midst of turmoil, will be reminded to "delete that and replace it". I hear the groan that means, "Please, can I just vent?" I remind them that venting is still our verbal instructions to the universe. If you must, go ahead and vent. I compare it to "word vomit", and like all vomit, we must quickly clean it up. It is in the word vomit that the energy and intention are spelled out to the universe. So, clean it up expeditiously and replace those instructions with higher vibrational word choices and happier emotions. Seek empowering thoughts and statements as well as emotions that feel better.

Let me walk you through some scenarios. One of my clients, Beth, knowing what she is thinking is disempowering but needing to share it in our session, will raise her hand in the ready position and say, "I delete this as I say it". While she is saying the statement she immediately deletes it in our Pac-Man style. Then she takes a deep breath and replaces the statement with one more empowering and holds onto the verbiage and the emotion of it. It is in the holding onto the energy of the new empowering belief that we begin the process of embracing it.

Another of my clients reported how her farm seemed to attract every sick or stray animal for miles around. She complained how high her vet bills were and how much time she spent taking care of all these creatures. She also commented how it must be her "lot in life" to be the caregiver for God's sick creatures because He keeps sending them to her. Do you see the connection? After I explained to her how her verbiage and her belief became the energy and intention for her farm, she was eager to change both. She began focusing her attention on raising happy and healthy goats and chickens. Within three months she had her ten acre farm filled with goats and chickens and had planted flowers and herbs. Her energy followed her thoughts. And last we spoke, not one new sick or stray creature had found its way to her farm.

A young mother came to see me because each of her children suffered with severe sinus infections with every season change. She repeated the statement many times at her introductory appointment. She said it with such determination I had no doubt she was accurate in her diagnosis. When I offered this concept of focusing her energy on what she wanted (healthy children) instead of what she didn't want (sinus infections) she said, "That's just nuts. They HAVE sinus infections every season. I can't just wish that way!" I smiled as we discussed actions to improve their immune system, procedures to reduce their exposure to germs, and health promoting foods. I ended with how our intention actually sets up the pathway for our future experiences and how our energy follows our thoughts. Because her children were clear of sinus infections at that moment, it was easy for her to reluctantly repeat, "My children are free of sinus issues". I recommended she repeat that statement at least three to five times each day, and with happy emotion since they were currently free of sinus issues. At the time of this writing, she and the children were through five season changes and had remained free of sinus infections. The mother says she has noticed she frequently catches herself saying or thinking other thoughts about how frustrating life can be. She cancels those and replaces them with more pleasant and positive statements. Every step forward is another step in the direction of your choosing - choose well!

While working with a family and their dog, I noticed the dog had a high level of energy and was easily distracted and seldom followed commands. While demonstrating how the dog responded to their commands (or didn't), I couldn't help but notice they also called the dog "stupid", "bonehead", and "brainless". When I asked about their nicknames for the dog, they explained he acted like he had no brain and he was just plain stupid. We discussed how energy follows our thoughts and how we can delete thoughts that no longer serve us (or the dog) and replace them with higher vibrational thoughts that better serve us (and the dog). I recommended they refrain from using derogatory descriptors and begin using words that describe how they would like the dog to be. This family had gotten into the habit of making fun of the dog. It was not an overnight transition. However, they made a compelling effort and with every little effort they put forth they noticed a slight improvement in the concentration and focus for the dog. Each slight improvement they noticed encouraged them to triumph. The cycle continued and although the dog remained high energy, was more focused and followed commands the majority of the time. When we pay attention to our intention, we see significant results.

Remember, I am a work in progress, too. This is one of my personal experiences about replacing thoughts with something of higher quality. Several years ago I was the administrator for a hospice company. I noticed about thirty percent of the staff had negative attitudes. It was evident they did not enjoy their jobs. I found myself saying "I am surrounded by people who hate their job". OOOOOOPS! Delete that. Replace it. I replaced it with, "I am surrounded by people who absolutely love their job!" I said it several times throughout the day and with great feeling and I smiled while I said it. I knew it would mean some changes were on the horizon.

I could be moved to a new position where everyone absolutely loved their job OR things would change in my office. Within three months, several of those with the negative attitudes had resigned and moved on. The remainder had found a new fondness for their position. It was incredible.

Several years ago, I noticed a few friends and family members were treating me with less respect and friendliness than I had hoped for. I began focusing on what I wanted. Several times a day I would say, "I am surrounded by people who love and respect me." Because I was eager for that love and respect to be fully realized, I focused my thoughts and energy and emotion into that affirmation and expected the universe to fully follow the direction. I certainly got what I asked for. New clients and workshop attendees began to appear. My business expanded and I felt the shift. However, the friends and family who were less than loving and respectful didn't become more loving and more respectful as I had hoped. They either stepped back or disappeared. Although I was not fully prepared for what transpired, it left me with the people who loved and respected me. There was more space for more people to step in who will love and respect me.

Do you see how beautifully the universe orchestrated that maneuver with finesse and efficiency? I asked to be surrounded by people who love and respect me. I got what I requested. I left the "how" open ended. I discovered there is no wiggle room for interpretation. My prayer was answered and for that, I am grateful! In retrospect, my intention was not accurately reflected in my request. Had I paid better attention to my intention, I may have asked for a higher level of love and respect from those in my life. That would have been more graceful and gentle on my spirit. I prefer all relationships to be about love and service to each other. I was anticipating a strengthening of those relationships to grow stronger and be wonderful. Well, I did get what I asked for, but it didn't come with pink sparkles, rainbows and unicorns. (Sad - I am quite fond of pink sparkles, rainbows and unicorns!)

Chapter 4

What is Your Intention?
Find Your Intention - Find Your Fuel

THE QUESTION I ASK MOST frequently of my clients and workshop attendees is: "What is your intention?" It is also, perhaps, the most difficult question for them to answer. Why? Because we seldom ask ourselves why we are doing something before we do it. We just do it. It's because it's something we've always done. Or it's something we are supposed to do. Or it is something that needs to be done and who else is going to do it. Or worse, it's a reaction to something or someone else.

As I observe and study human behavior, I am intrigued by the activities and actions we participate in simply because - we just do! Without intention, we are like the little silver ball inside the pinball machine of life. Bouncing around from one bumper to another (life events) and occasionally being batted at by someone trying to change our direction for us. I lived that version of life. My pinball machine was called Spitler's Law and it was, like all pinball machines, quite an obnoxious and very colorful spectacle.

Intention drives everything we do. If we are not fully aware of what our intention is and we are just going through the motions, then we are living life without awareness of our intention. Living life without focus and direction means we are most likely not enjoying it either. One day is just like another and we wonder if this is truly all there is to our life. Some people call this depression. Some call it boredom. I will offer a different perspective. Rather than focusing on what it is or what to call it, focus on making it better! Since intention drives everything we do - let's make a conscious choice to become aware of why we do what we do and why we think what we think. Let's *make it intentional*. Let's shine the spotlight on our intention and see what is really there. Then let's clean it up, give it our attention, change its direction and attain a higher quality focus. As our energy follows our thoughts, we will certainly have more meaning and more value to what we do and how we do it. It will make sense to us why we choose what we do. If it doesn't make sense for us to be doing it - why are we doing it? When we pay attention to our intention we see what we didn't see before and we understand more.

Probably the most profound question to ask yourself about any action you take or reaction you make is, "What is my intention?" It's best to ask yourself before you actually take on the task or action or formulate your reaction. However, if you have already completed the proposition before you have begun to probe for your intention, you will just ask yourself "What *was* my intention?" Either way, you will most likely be surprised by what you discover about yourself with this inquiry. You make take steps to amend the action or resolve the reaction.

I remember a client, Sandra, who complained bitterly about her husband. He was, in her eyes, incompetent, sloppy, thoughtless and often rude. She complained it was time for a formal intervention. She had already determined who she wanted at the event and how it should transpire. I listened intently as I am aware the type of intervention she was referring to was generally used for alcoholics and addicts in an effort to get them into immediate rehab. The usual participants are those who are most profoundly affected by the behavior of the person for whom the intervention is planned. However, Sandra had created a team of her supporters for this event. She was planning to surround her husband with those who agree with her but who were not at all directly affected by his behavior. In fact, those closest to him were either not to be invited to the intervention or did not support an intervention.

When Sandra was finished, I asked her what was her intention in crafting this intervention for her husband. She danced around the answer, so I asked again. She danced again; I asked again. Her answers were about her issue with his behavior toward her. Her answers indicated how her life would be better if he would be nicer to her. Her final answer had absolutely nothing to do with the husband and any personal benefit for him. Her intention was to have him called out by her peers so he could see how his behavior was affecting her. She became aware of her intention and was able to see how her focus was about how he frustrated her so! As her cycle of energy following thoughts continued, he became more frustrating to her, and there were more thoughts of how frustrating he was and … and… and… and the cycle continued in her frustration.

I recommended she put the intervention idea on hold and consider a few less intense possibilities. Together we crafted a written list of what she really wanted from her husband and from the relationship as she moved forward. It was a wonderful list of qualities most wives wish for from their spouses. She was absolutely confident he couldn't meet any of them! However, she acquiesced and even adopted the motto, "I'll fake it till I make it". She agreed to pick just the top five qualities to focus on each week. She would think of him, smile and say to herself how wonderful it was that her husband had these fine qualities. I also recommended she remember when he demonstrated those qualities in the past.

She reported back after the first week. She said she felt absolutely ridiculous doing this activity and found herself chuckling about it throughout the day. She said she also noticed how many times a day she caught herself thinking contrary thoughts she had to cancel and delete. She said THAT was the more challenging work! She also said there was no difference in her husband. However, in further conversation she mentioned they had played cards together and both had belly-laughed! She said she could not remember the last time that happened. Hummm...... I saw that as improvement! Each week Sandra reported some level of improvement. She also had noticed how frequently she had stinkin' thinkin' thoughts about so many other things. She said, "Good grief! I cancel and delete more of what I say than I keep! I had no idea I was so negative". (Bonus!) The ripple effect of making it intentional is amazing! It just keeps on going. And, as you may have guessed, the situation with Sandra's husband improved. She found how focusing on what she wanted actually brought what she wanted into being. The better at this concept she was, the more of what she wanted manifested. Her husband thinks Sandra is happy and that makes him happy. Together they are beginning to travel. Something they have always wanted to do but felt too financially squeezed to do. When they used the concepts described in this book together to focus on being able to travel, they found the finances and the time to travel.

Imagine what you may discover about yourself with a little exploration and investigation into the intention behind your actions and reactions. As so often happens, our true intention has little to do with what we think it does. Delving deeper into our thoughts and intentions often leads us to either a place we didn't know existed or to old emotional wounds needing resolution and healing. This process of delving deeper is also quite helpful for children. Help them to pay attention to their intention. As we ask them to explore the underlying thoughts behind their actions, we are often surprised at what we learn. We may have to probe a bit past the first exchange as the outcome there is often, "I don't know" or an explanation of how someone else made them do it.

Probing deeper, we often discover the child is just hoping to catch some attention and love. Other times we have discovered a hurt that goes too deep and is covered up with anger. Now, remember, we are not asking "why" questions. Those are much too confrontational and often are met with irritation or anger. Asking "what was your intention?" opens up a conversation. Though it may cause come confoundedness, it will result in an explorational journey which usually has a positive outcome. When a child (or client of any age) responds with the proverbial, "I don't know." I respond with something like, "Sure you do." Or "At some level we all know why we do what we do." I smile with a knowing and encouraging (but non-judgmental) nod and I ask again. The answer is important, both to me as a practitioner and to them as a human being. When the child is too young to understand the word intention, we choose other words to help him or her examine the meaning behind their actions. You may ask them, "Are you trying to be helpful or hurtful." "What was the purpose of..." or "What did you hope would happen when you....." Each question will open up a journey of self discovery.

Zak, an 8 year old boy, reached over and snatched a toy out of his younger brother's hand. The younger brother cried while Zak walked away with the toy he had no interest in just moments earlier. I asked Zak, "What did you hope would happen when you took the toy from Ken?" He wrinkled up his whole face as he said, "what?" I calmly asked him again while noticing his parents were watching closely. Zak was somewhat befuddled. He said, "I don't know what you mean." I re framed with, "You said to yourself - I'm going to get that toy from Ken and ….." He gave a heavy sigh and said, "Fine, I'll give it back". Interesting! No scolding. No shouting. No fussing. He gave it back at his own choosing. Why? I'm not exactly certain, but I believe that during the exploration process, he found the reason he took the toy and preferred not to share it. That's fine! He explored. He discovered. He made a better choice. Perhaps he discovered he had no idea why he took the toy so giving it back made sense to him. Parenting is all about consistency. With consistency in exploring his true intentions, he will find more suitable options to act on or he will find appropriate ways to share what he is thinking. Remember, there is no judgment. There was no scolding, no punishment and no directive to give it back. He made that decision on his own.

Carla is a middle-aged woman who came to me for career coaching. She was frustrated with her current job and was looking for something new. We worked a plan where she identified all the elements of a job she wanted and would focus her thoughts on having a job with these wanted elements. About half way through the session, I felt as if she wanted to be in a completely different industry. Her verbiage was such that changing jobs in the same field may have helped her for a while but certainly would not have made her heart sing. I asked her what her intention was in moving to a new position. She said all the right things and many coaches would have just moved on in the session. I probed for more. I asked, "If money were no object and you could do anything you wanted to do, what would it be?" She burst into tears. Her intention in moving to a new position was in hopes it would buy her more time to invest into her retirement system. She despised her job and knew the next job would be no better but hoped a new job with new people would make it easier for her to wait it out a few more years. Now we had something tangible to work with.

Her true intention revealed, we could move forward with a plan on how to focus her thoughts to make this a positive experience and allow her energy to be flowing in the direction of forward movement. Daily she expressed how important this job is in allowing her financial freedom in just four years. She expressed gratitude for having this job (which she did very well by the way) and how easily and effortlessly it was to continue working for the next four or even six years. The following week she reported her anxiety was gone! Her depression was only 10 percent better, but certainly improved. And, she felt she could see the light at the end of the tunnel. Without examining her true intention for a job change, she may very well have changed positions and taken on all the unnecessary stress which comes with a job change and she most likely would have continued with the same frustrations and stress. Instead, she was able to identify her deeper desire (to find a way to make it another four years) and developed a positive plan to get her there. Along the way, she was able to reduce depression and relieve anxiety and find some fulfillment in her work again. This was a process of discovery with slow but steady improvements. Every day became better. (Bonus!)

As you can imagine, I question my own intention often. I mentioned in the previous chapter, this is an ongoing process of personal growth and development. To do it well, we do it persistently and we improve as we go. Some years ago, I realized my husband and I were going along well together but he just didn't seem as attentive as he had in the past. I began to notice how seldom he complimented me. He would walk beside me but not reach for my hand. As I was noticing all the things he wasn't doing, I was inadvertently focusing my thoughts and energy (intention) into what he wasn't doing and what I did not want - which was even less attention and affection. Then I had the epiphany! To get more of what I wanted, his love, attention and affection, I would do well to express more love, attention and affection. I knew to focus my attention and energy (intention) on everything he did to show love, attention and affection. Silly girl! You know how this works, so do it!

Immediately I made a conscious choice to feel more loved and valued. I also made the decision I would be for him what I wanted from him. At that moment, I called him at work. I left a voice mail with a sweet and happy voice, saying simply, "Hi handsome! Just wanted to let you know I was thinking of you and smiling. I love you." And from that moment, I was on a mission to show him all the attention and affection I wanted. (Remember, we focus our attention on what we want not what we don't want.) I wanted a Damn-Near-Perfect husband so I decided he already was! I called him Damn

Near Perfect and I still do. I shared with him my intention behind this mission. He raised his eyebrows and chuckled. He was happy to hear he would be the recipient of positive attention. He laughed when I called him Damn Near Perfect. He said he knew he wasn't. I knew it too. It didn't matter. The critical element was that I wanted him to be Damn Near Perfect in my eyes so my eyes needed to see him as such. I wanted to have lots of love and affection from him, so I needed to be the catalyst that ignited that fire. The more I gave, the more I received. It didn't happen overnight. It was an unfolding; it was worth every effort.

When we celebrated our 30th wedding anniversary, we had a small ceremony we called our vow renewal. We had written our original vows so it made sense we would do it again for the renewal. It was just the two of us in that gazebo so we were free to say whatever we needed to say. The ceremony was more like a series of "I'm sorry" and "Thank you" statements, but it was a wonderful recognition of our history and a beautiful tribute to our present and future. The intention we share today is not the same as it was ten years ago. It is nothing like it was twenty years ago. Thirty years ago we didn't know what the word intention meant! Our current intention is to make certain our spouse knows exactly how deeply they are loved, how profoundly proud we are of who we have become together, and how precious we see the spirit in each other. This intention truly drives our actions and reactions.

All humans want to be loved and valued. We all desire at some level to give and receive affection and share our love. When we withhold our love from another, we must explore our intention for withholding. The more we understand our intention, the more we realize how the withholding makes us feel. There is always a true intention hidden in the act of withholding. Find your intention and you find your fuel. Set your intention and you will see results.

Chapter 5
Make it Intentional
Living Life With Purpose

I HEAR IT OFTEN, "ITS ALL part of the plan." Or "There is a reason for everything." More frequently (and my favorite), "Everything happens for a reason." These statements usually follow an unfavorable event of some sort. Someone doesn't get the job they interviewed for and someone else offers up "there is a reason for everything." Somehow that is supposed to make the situation better. However, it also supports the idea that we have no ability to impact our future and it's all up to God or the universe. Here comes the virtual pinball machine of life again. In this theory, God has control of the flipper buttons.

Humans were given free will. We make decisions every day that mess up the proverbial plan. Every decision we make can bring us closer to or farther from the life plan we choose before we were born. We can make a dozen choices which take us farther from the life plan and then, with one opportunity presented to us, we can make a choice that brings us right back to the plan. That's one of the wonderful gifts of this universe. We have choices, options, and opportunities, and the free will to act upon them.

If everything was part of the plan, there would be no need for free will. There would be no choices offered and no opportunities given. Why? If everything was part of the plan, the choices would be preprogrammed like instinct. We would go about our lives living out a perfectly programmed plan. We would, in a sense, be acting out a play in which the plot, the scripting, the scene changes and the ending are already written. We make dozens of decisions and choices every day. Each choice has an outcome. It is either a reward or a consequence. Some choices lead us in one direction while another choice will lead us in a completely different direction. We get to choose. We have the opportunity to experience life in any way we desire. That's the beauty of free will. However, it is also the challenge of free will.

The reason things happen to and for us is because we make decisions and take actions everyday which impact our present and our future. We choose it. We made the decisions and took the actions that led us to be right where we are. Taking no purposeful action is a decision to allow the pinball machine to fire up and act for us. Does that sound like a good plan to you? Who is standing at the flipper buttons waiting to take a whack at you?

For those who believe everything is simply part of the plan, how do you explain the opportunities and choices that come to us? A lady in one workshop offered up this explanation: "God knows which choice we will make so the plan is already prepared for us." Another said, "Those are not really choices. They are planted in our path to make us think, but ultimately every decision we make is part of our life plan." Another offered this idea, "Every choice is really a directional guarantee from either God or Satan." That comment brought forth a great deal of discussion among the workshop participants.

I will offer a different perspective. I agree that every decision we make becomes a part of our life plan. I do not, however, believe every decision we make is already predestined and predetermined for us. Again, why have free will? With every choice we make, the universe is ready and waiting to arrange situations, people, and circumstances in order to answer our intention (or lack thereof). Like GPS, situations will be recalculated to either restore you in the direction toward your chosen life purpose or allow you to move yourself away from it. Simply put, whether we do it intentionally or not, every day we are engaging with the universe to give us what we are focusing on. For those allowing the pinball machine of life to move and influence them, they become easily shifted by the universe to help others achieve their focus. We are either in process of experiencing our own life lessons, goals, and spiritual growth or we are participating in the lessons and development of another. Within the unfocused or unintentional life, one can be moved and shifted or left to stagnate. It depends on what's happening in the energy around you. But when you *make it intentional,* you are either mindfully putting in the requests with your focused thoughts or consciously choosing to engage in this creative process. You are purposely paying attention to your intention. That's when the happiness happens and magical moments manifest.

Occasionally, people lose their focus and spend time experiencing drugs or alcohol. They might participate in activities like gambling, prostitution, theft, violence and other behaviors that distract them from their life purpose. Even then, the universe is still with them and available to them every moment of every day. These people will have a strong knowing their actions are not in their own best interest. Still, they choose to continue. They may have a desire to stop the behaviors. They may genuinely want to stop for their own benefit or for the benefit of others. Yet, they either feel they cannot stop or simply choose not to stop. The universe will be responding to their choice to continue. The universe is continually adjusting in an attempt to guide them back to their life purpose, while honoring their free will decisions to continue their current lifestyle behaviors.

Our feelings and our emotions are our inner guidance system. Those gut feelings tell us that we are on or off our true life path. Those internal signs are our intuition. Some say our gut feelings are our Guardian Angels letting us know we are off our life path and changes are needed. We may get gentle nudges. Sometimes we get great big messages. (I'd refrain from asking to be hit upside the head with messages, though!) It remains our free will choice how we respond. Thankfully, we have the opportunity to change our thoughts, behaviors, patterns, beliefs and decisions every moment of every day. We can recreate ourselves, our present situation and our future circumstances by paying attention to our intention, and making the decision to *make it intentional* and push the reset button of our life.

There are those people who put themselves in positions where they don't have to make choices. They may get into partnerships with people who are controlling or domineering and who make the decisions for them. There are interesting dynamics at play in these situations. They can blame their partners for any outcomes they deem unfavorable. They can refrain from having to choose, thus they are able to say they have no opportunity to change their life. "Woe is me! I am a victim of the life circumstances surrounding me." In fact, it's all very clear. They have chosen to ride the silver ball in the pinball machine of life. They have allowed others to determine their direction in life rather than creating their own life path. They have disempowered themselves. Being disempowered is a choice, too.

Now it is appropriate to discuss how to empower ourselves. How do we apply the delete and re-think it concept with intention and activate it in our everyday life? How can we come from the disempowered feelings of weakness and angst to the strength and confidence empowerment brings? Everyone has the capability to do it. It will take time and some effort; everyone will reap the benefits from the investment.

Since we know our thoughts are the things that create our life, we also know we are literally manifesting our reality with every thought we think and everything we say and do. We are manifesting at the speed of thought - literally! So, to manifest well, we must think empowering thoughts. To think empowering thoughts we have to… well… think good and empowering thoughts. Isn't that easy enough?

When we think a thought that is disempowering, (and we all do it) just delete it and have a momentary do-over. Do-Over's are appropriate and positively encouraged. A do-over allows us to change the energy of the whole process. Just being aware of our intention makes a significant difference. However, a do-over releases the energy of the old thought pattern just deleted and replaces it with the energy of the new thought we are wanting to embrace. Do-Over's are the bomb! We are paying attention to our intention and we are proactively pursuing positive progress.

It takes little more than a minute to change your whole energy field to the new vibration of what you are wanting. It's a moment well spent to bring about new life to your vision. When we engage in a do-over, we are doing it with purpose and making it an intentional act. That's the name of the whole process: "**Make it Intentional.**"

I frequently use the phrase, "Set your intention for what you want, not what you don't want." I often hear people sarcastically saying how they know what the outcome of an upcoming event will be. They may be referring to how stressful a meeting will be or how an interview will turn out. Maybe they are simply talking about how they will never find that great dress for an upcoming party. I've heard thousands of comments like these and each time I cringe. They are inadvertently calling their attention to what they don't want. I recommend they set their intention for what they do want to happen, not what they don't want. I've heard all the reasons why they said what they said. I hear how they didn't really mean it that way. I've heard, "You just don't understand." (Oh, yes I do!) To each one I again recommend they delete, cancel or remove the energy of those thoughts, set their intention for what they want and focus their attention to the outcome they seek. Sometimes people will continue on defending their limiting belief. They have free will and I am a good listener, so I wait them out. However, my viewpoint remains the same. Instead of arguing for your limitations, open wide the possibilities before you and see what may happen for you. It's not difficult and requires nothing more than a vested interest in your present and your future.

Setting your intention entails looking ahead at the activity you are about to engage in and thinking about what you want the outcome to be. Once you are clear on what outcome you truly want to have happen, change the energy, intention and emotion from desire, to belief and expectation. Yes, I said expectation. Meaning - expect you will get what you ask for. Your words are prayers, remember? They are instructions to the universe. So, expect you will get what you request. Where your attention goes, your intention flows, thus your focused thoughts will follow. Where your thoughts are, your energy follows.

When you think you have no desire or wanting, you will still call forth what you've asked for. I'll explain what I mean. Want nothing and you will either receive nothing or you will receive whatever the pinball machine of life flips at you. Every human being has a desire for something. When a client tells me there is nothing they want, I know better. I probe deeper. There is always something wanted to support a core value. Even a recluse has a desire for seclusion. Being aware of the desire gives us the ability to be proactive in focusing our attention and intention upon it.

When there is a wanting but no energy and attention flowing towards it, the wanting becomes as meaningless as wishing to find a job and never applying for one. Or wanting to win a race but not running it. Or hoping your car starts but never putting gas in it. (The illustrations are endless.)

You have set your intention for what you want and have increased your energy, attention and positive emotions towards it. Next, verbalize the expectation in words that you can continue to embrace. Call it an affirmation or a mantra and refer to it often and with energy and positive emotion. Delete any thoughts or fears that sneak their way up to the surface that may deter you from your desired goal. Cancel any comments that may actually make it out of your mouth before you can catch, delete and replace them. Remember, this is an ongoing process, so make it your mission to do it and do it well. You will reap the rewards quickly. It is the awareness and the desire to do this process that is essential and it is putting it into action and practicing it that presents the best outcomes. Like any talent or skill, establishing a consistent practice makes it better.

When my son was planning a move across the country, he was looking for a new job and he became easily frustrated. He knew what he wanted but was losing his patience waiting for the right job. Fear was also beginning to set in for him in this process. We had daily conversations about his options, his impatience, his focus, and where he would do well to focus his thoughts and energy. He knew to set his intention for what he wanted and he knew to keep his energy focused there. He also knew he had to be a good human and do the human parts of this process too. He applied for many different positions. Some jobs he applied for were nothing at all what he wanted but he was aware there is often a great potential in the interview process. Additionally, he had become fearful and he was, at that point, willing to take just about anything.

What he really wanted was for his current employer, a large, international travel company, to create an opportunity for him to work from home. Although he would be many states away from the call center, working the phones from home could be set up easily. When that possibility did not manifest, his second preference was for a position with the local city ballet company. He was teaching some classes there already, knew the staff, and felt comfortable. However, they had no open positions. I encouraged him to set his intention to something like, "Very soon, I will be working for the ballet." He was flustered because there was no open position. He reminded me they couldn't just fabricate a position and no one was looking for other work. I reminded him to take on the motto of "fake it till you make it" and to focus his energy and attention to working for the ballet. A few weeks later he accepted a position with a prestigious hotel. It wasn't the position he had hoped for but he needed a job and sensed he shouldn't wait any longer. Knowing his intention, I suggested he perform well at this job and allow it to catapult him forward into a greater position. But secretly, I was disappointed for him. I knew he had desperately wanted to stay with the travel company and in lieu of that, he wanted to work with the ballet. But I also know patience is not his greatest virtue.

Two days after he started at the hotel, the ballet company contacted him. They had an unexpected early retirement announced and wanted him for the job. He was elated. The hotel staff was disappointed but understood and appreciated his candor and honesty. Two weeks after he started with the ballet, there was an unexpected resignation and they moved him into a higher ranking position to which he was even more aligned. He couldn't have been happier! Later, I learned he had never really given up his desire to work from home with the travel company. I learned this when they called him, six months after he had moved across the country, and offered an opportunity for him to work with them from home. Again, he was elated! Yet, his time with the ballet company had been wonderful and he was conflicted. However, when he spoke about the travel company, his face lit up. That was all the evidence needed to know where his heart belonged. He gave the ballet company a lengthy notice and went with the travel company. He was on their leader board again within a month. Even though he had resigned himself to the understanding the position couldn't be created for him, his thoughts and energy, coupled with the emotion of true desire, continued to flow. It took some time for the universe to adjust, but it did. Patience, determination, expectation and confidence are very valuable tools for this process.

I work with a large clientele for career and performance coaching. There are always special projects and upcoming meetings or events for which my clients are preparing. One of my clients, Jill, shared with me her horror stories of how the annual meeting for her company has always been her responsibility to prepare, organize and manage. She told me that no matter how well it is organized, two directors always manage to completely mess it up. Armed with the knowledge and understanding of how to set intention, expect the desired outcome, and focus her energy and attention towards the outcome expected, she set forth with a new attitude. Jill reported that she had set her intention that the meeting would be well organized, well attended and all in attendance would have their preparations complete and the agenda would be followed.

For four weeks she repeated the intention and when someone would make a snide comment about those two directors, my client would wave her hand, delete those comments and replace them with statements about how they would have all their prep work done and the meeting would go right down the agenda as planned. She was met with a lot of giggles but she managed to engage a few others in her focused attention for a better outcome. To the amazement of many of the staff members, the meeting went off without a hitch or a glitch or even a hint of a problem. After the meeting, Jill was congratulated by the directors and the board members for having done such a great job at the meeting. She also received a nice bonus! (BONUS!)

Karen is another client who had taken on the job of coaching a freshman volleyball team. Barely out of high school herself, Karen was younger than their previous coach. Before the season started she was nervous and even anxious about how to communicate with the young girls and how they might respond to her coaching skills. She was equally anxious how the parents might perceive her because she was so young. First we worked on her confidence about her skills and knowledge. Then we crafted the plan.

We started with being clear on her intention for each of those issues: communication with the team members, support for the team members, and parents' perception. She found it easy to speak about and visualize the outcomes she wanted. She was able to feel the emotions of pride and happiness while she visualized the outcomes. Her obstacle was her fear that this was all imaginary. I asked her to trust the process, since she had nothing to lose and everything to gain. She seemed agreeable and we wrote the affirmations that supported the outcomes she desired. She focused her attention on her intention and her energy followed. She decided to have some fun with the process, which amplified the energy and emotions.

As the season started, her confidence was solid. She called a meeting with the parents the first week of the season. She had created handouts for them, along with a page of Frequently Asked Questions. She won them over by being forthright, organized, and accessible. The team responded just as she had visualized. They worked hard, they played well and they stayed upbeat even when they lost. She absolutely loved her experience. She became a huge supporter of "delete, delete, delete" and shared it with the girls on the team. She taught them the concepts of how energy follows thought and set your intention for what you want, not what you don't want. Those kids are learning skills that extend far beyond the volleyball court. (Bonus!)

If it feels right, do it

A very unhappy man spoke out at one of my workshops. He told me he thought this whole process was ridiculous. He said, "It's all part of the plan and we are supposed to let go and let God." The discussion that followed went something like this:

Me: Tell me more about what you mean?

Him: We are always right where we are supposed to be.

Me: I offer to you, you are right where you choose to be.

Him: No! Where we are is right where we are supposed to be. It's part of the plan.

Me: The plan? To which plan do you refer?

Him: The divine plan. You know the one that God put together for us to follow.

Me: (Setting my intention we reach a good place easily, effortlessly and quickly) you know about free will, right? God gave us free will. So we have the freedom to choose our actions and reactions to nearly everything. As a matter of fact, I submit to you, we mess up that divine plan quite frequently and I am certain the divine realm scrambles daily to adjust… you know….like the GPS does when we take a different turn than the one the GPS recommended. It adjusts.

Him: So you're saying we should just throw out the master plan and do our own thing? That's blasphemy!

Me: (Setting my intention he hear with open heart and mind and I speak as guided) I gently asked him if he chose his clothing for today.

Him: (Smirking) yes

Me: You have a closet full of clothes from which to choose, right? Did you choose which direction you drove here tonight?

Him: (Impatiently) yes

Me: Yet, you could have changed direction at any time, right? Did you choose to speak up when you did?

Him: (Laughing) yes

Me: But you could have remained silent or left the room. Do you suppose those 3 things are part of the master plan?

Him: (Pondering) Yes.... No....I don't know. Maybe not those little things.

Me: So, let's consider that there certainly is a divine plan, and we, without doubt, have free will.

Him: Okay......

Me: If everything is all part of the master plan, why would we be given free will? Why give human beings the opportunity to choose some things for ourselves but not others.

Him: (Pondering in silence)

Me: You agree we have free will, right?

Him: Yes

Me: Is there a dividing line between what we can and cannot choose? Do you believe we make mistakes in some of our choices with that free will?

Him: (Nodding in a big way) Oh Yes!

Me: And we live the outcome of those choices, right? Consequences or reward, right?

Him: Right.

Me: If we make a choice that takes us away from the master plan, how would we know?

Him: (sigh) I don't know

Me: (Looking around the room) Does anyone want to guess? How might Spirit guide us to know if we have made a big mistake and jumped off the master plan or even if we have made a choice that leads us away from our divine life purpose? Like... took on a business partner that wasn't for our best or moved to a foreign country on a whim...

(Shouted from the back of the room) - We would feel it!

Me: Absolutely! We will feel it. Usually, right here in our gut! Our emotions are our compass. When we are feeling everything is right with our world, it most likely is. When we are feeling something is just not right, it most likely is. When things seem out of balance, they are.

This theory, "If it feels right, do it" and the conversation I shared, is more about trusting our inner wisdom. Our inner knowing guides us to what is right, healthy, helpful and healing versus what is unsettling, distressing, troublesome or out of balance. "If it feels right, do it" isn't about a momentary feeling for fun or frolic. It's about a deeper knowing when you are right on track or that you are right where you really want to be. We, unquestionably, want to be on the path of our life purpose. When we are on path, we feel delighted. When we are close, we will feel connected and confident. When we are off path, we feel anxious, upset, disengaged, depressed, desperation or despair.

Now, keep in mind, you do not now nor do you ever have to set your intention for anything. You can play virtual pinball with your life. You have free will. You choose. Just remember, when you do not purposely set your intention for what you want, then you will be just like that little silver ball in the pinball machine just winging it through life being bounced around willy-nilly, hither and yon, experiencing whatever comes along. If you're choosing that lifestyle now, how's it working for ya? Our thoughts bring to us our experiences whether we are consciously choosing them or not. Would you rather be fully aware of what's coming to you by your thoughts, energy and attention or would you rather be surprised? Paying attention to your intention means you become aware of what you are consciously and subconsciously thinking. Without purposeful intention setting, you are allowing your subconscious thoughts and your old beliefs to guide your journey. Would you rather be the driver of your life-purpose bus or just ride along in the back seat?

As you pay attention and purposely set your intention, you may be surprised how often your old beliefs materialize. You may be equally surprised how the old patterns no longer serve you. Those patterns and beliefs become excess weight; they keep us tied to our past. They keep us from experiencing the *more* available to us. When we identify them and change them, we are free to soar.

There are those who will continue to mosey on through life being kicked around and knocked down. They prefer to blame their circumstances on life itself or someone else, rather than wonder what they could possibly do differently to affect an altered outcome. You see, it is much easier to whine and complain about our circumstance than it is to: stop, explore deeper, step forward and empower ourselves to change them. Being a victim of others means we have no accountability to or responsibility for where we find ourselves.

I'm sure you know people who are constantly lamenting about their life and the circumstances surrounding them. They complain how miserable everything is and how they try and try and try and nothing seems to work out for them. Yep - it's a common affliction that causes emotional pain, distress, grief, depression, hardship and almost always leads to illness and adversity. It's sad and utterly unnecessary.

Embark upon this journey of discovering positive perspectives and invest even a moderate amount of effort, you will soon notice enough improvement to continue learning and working the processes. As you notice the improvements, you may be more willing to put forth added energy and attention into the process. The cycle of improvement and higher quality outcomes will continue. You will experience more pleasant emotions. You will feel stronger and more confident. You will begin to seek more ways to enhance your progress. You will be living your life with purpose.

Chapter 6
A Purposeful Positive Perspective
How to Find it and Keep it

L ET'S TAKE A DEEPER LOOK at how our perspective changes when we realize we have the power to create our reality. This chapter focuses on the power we have and how to use it wisely. Yes, it means we will be earnestly and vigorously keeping our thoughts in a positive perspective. It means being aware when we stray into negative thoughts of self or others and changing those thoughts to a more positive perspective – purposely, intentionally, ardently, energetically, enthusiastically and with expectation for our desired outcome. It means being consistent in looking for a better way to process and think about the happenings in our life.

Those moments when our perspective is glum, frustrated, or perhaps even anxious or depressed, we will actively pursue a path towards higher vibrational thoughts and feelings. We will focus on a brighter and more positive perspective. The goal is to make it as much a part of our day as brushing our teeth, watching where we step, organizing our work space, or brushing lint off our clothing. Notice, each of those activities requires conscious thought, awareness and purpose. We notice something is askew and we realign it. We notice we have lint on our sleeve and we remove it. We use this same process with our thinking. When we notice something is askew or out of alignment with what we truly want or desire, then let's realign it. It is as simple as that!

We are human and subject to human emotions, fears, and frustrations. Thus we will have thoughts that are not always pleasant or positive. Be on the look out and become aware of them - then delete them. When you have thoughts that are unproductive - delete them. When you have thoughts that are negative or hurtful to self or others - delete them. Delete and re-think it. Delete the thoughts and then intentionally replace them with something more positive, more helpful, more productive, or more pleasant. Remember, this process is for our thoughts, spoken statements, written verbiage or feelings that do not feel right to us. Delete what is out of alignment or hurtful and replace it with something healthy, helpful, and healing. Remove what is disempowering and takes you out of balance and replace it with empowering thoughts more aligned with your true desire and your true nature.

In my workshops, we explore the process of deleting thoughts and statements quite thoroughly. We are also animated and often chuckle at the process. Participants in the workshops have some great visuals and actions for deleting disempowering thoughts and statements. I use my Pac-Man-style gesture. You may do this in whatever method works best for you. Deleting unproductive thoughts and statements can be as easy as thinking to yourself "delete that." Or you can be as creative as you desire. One participant visualized the words of the thought as if they were written on a computer screen. He then watched as the virtual cursor backspaced over the verbiage and visually deleted it. Another participant visualized the whole comment as if it was in a cartoon cloud and would see the verbiage in the cloud disappear, leaving a blank space inside the cloud. At the same workshop, upon hearing the description of the cartoon cloud, another woman said she had the same visualization but for her, the cloud disappeared. Your ability to delete the statements is as varied as your creativity allows.

It is not, however, to be taken lightly. We are not whimsically saying "delete that" without motive. Our intention is to literally delete the disempowering thought and the energy that comes with it. Then, replace it with something more meaningful and empowering. Your intention in this process guides it to completion.

Deleting the disempowering or unproductive thought or statement is the first step of the two step process. It initially involves our awareness of the thought (which may have become a written or spoken statement) and the action of deleting it along with the energy and emotion associated with it.

A friend of mine once told me it was too hard to constantly be on the look out for negative or pessimistic thoughts. I pondered for a moment and then asked her if it was too hard for her to do her personal hygiene, too? We laughed as we bantered back and forth. Her point was that we are conditioned to do some things so frequently we are able to do them absentmindedly. She's right. It doesn't take too much concentrated thought to brush and floss our teeth, or to wash our hands and face or sweep the floor. However, for every task we perform, we had to learn how to execute it properly. Initially, it was difficult to brush and floss our teeth or sweep the floor. Do you remember? It was only after we mastered the task that it became easy and routine. We can do dozens of tasks without much purposeful thought or focused attention. So many of these tasks, though, are done often enough if we miss something (a cobweb in the corner or a dust bunny behind the lamp) we can catch it the next time.

Isn't it interesting how much more focused our attention is on these same tasks if we are preparing for a special event? Think back to the last time you attended to a special occasion. Chances are you were more attentive to your hygiene, clothes, and overall look than you might have been for a casual gathering at home. Remember the last time you had guests over to the house? I'll bet you were much more attentive to the tasks of dusting, sweeping and clearing clutter than you would have been if no guests were expected.

The process of living life is much the same. We can progress through weeks or months of life with little focused attention and get by just fine. Then something comes up that is important enough to capture our attention and we either feel anxious or eager about the event's arrival. The more anxiety we feel about the event, the more dramatic or traumatizing the event could be. The more eager we are for the event, the more engaged or preoccupied we may be with it. Each of these has a sense of imbalance to it that, in turn, allows us to shift out of balance too. It's another great example of the pinball machine analogy.

Absentmindedly living life leaves us feeling disempowered, unfocused, or just plain bored. Absentmindedly doing our daily tasks is often when our subconscious mind brings up those pesky little disempowering and pessimistic thoughts. Being conscious and mindful of our thoughts, feelings and statements is where this process begins. Actively conquering and modifying them with positive perspectives becomes incredibly empowering, frees our spirit and helps us heal.

The second half of the process is perhaps the most challenging to a novice. Re-think it. It is the act of replacing the old belief, unproductive thought or statement with an improved and empowering thought or statement. We re-think it. If you have been in a pattern of feeling negativity about self or others for quite some time, this will be an interesting challenge for you. It could be difficult, perhaps, because you haven't been focused on positive perspectives. Initially, you may find this arduous or painful, as if you are fighting an uphill battle. But keep up the practice because you will find it gets easier and becomes much more fun the more often you do it. Remember, this is an ever-evolving, continual process of self-discovery and improvement. The process is a tool to be used faithfully. The more we use the tool, the sharper our skill.

I've said before, it's not always easy. The first few attempts at riding a bicycle weren't easy either. It is our determination to reach the desired goal (living life with purpose) that carries us through the choppy waters. You may discover this technique to be more problematic when emotions are high. It may feel impossible to delete and re-think it while being screamed at or experiencing pain. Deleting disempowering thoughts while annoyed or angry means we must refocus our attention to see our genuine intention. Often just the activity of refocusing allows for a diffusing of our emotions and the situation. (Bonus!)

One of the fun things about having social media is reading about fabulous ways to make our everyday tasks so much simpler, or better yet, ways to simplify things we hadn't ever even thought about. I've seen videos and photos on how to simplify everything from cutting watermelon and avocados to packing clothes, folding sheets, and making lemonade. We do so many tasks or perform so many processes by rote. Our grandparents taught our parents and our parents taught us. We do the task or perform the process just as we were taught and focus little further thought on it. Folding T-shirts is a good example. We learn, we do, we move on. Twenty years later, someone on social media creates a video which shows us a fabulous new way to fold T-shirts and WOW! Our world has expanded!

Make it Intentional has the same effect. We have been thinking and behaving as we have been trained to do. Maybe it was through trial and error we found a way that worked for us and we just keep doing it the same way because it works. Suggesting you pay attention to your intention and make efforts to purposefully create your journey into something you want to experience, allows for your personal and spiritual growth. Your life becomes easier, more enjoyable and more fulfilling. Both your personal world and your world view will expand.

———— ⬥⬥⬥ ————

The process I am describing in this book provides us with the opportunity for a lifestyle change. The personal growth and self expansion creates a ripple effect that is immense. The ripple effect positively impacts us from our immediate circle of influence and expands outward to positively impact our entire world. That's why I most prefer the Purposeful Positive Perspective (the "Triple P") Approach.

When we are purposefully focused on our desired outcome, we have a positive expectation about it happening. Being positive rather than pessimistic about it means we bring a higher vibration of energy towards it and our energy follows our thoughts. Perspective is our frame of reference, our viewpoint, our attitude or our outlook. A positive perspective means a more positive pathway toward the outcome.

Often in session or workshops, I offer up different perspectives for the individual to use since their own viewpoint may be limited. A limited viewpoint means they typically see limited angles, aspects or opportunities. I hope to broaden their vantage point to allow for a more expanded view. Being offered a different perspective is much the same as being offered the opportunity to look at something through binoculars or a panoramic camera lens. We may be looking the in same direction but our observations or the views, are completely different.

Go to any accident scene and ask the witnesses to tell you what they observed. If you have twenty-five witnesses you will have twenty-five stories with varied elements. No two views will be exactly alike. The vantage points will have been different as will the perspectives of the witnesses depending upon their own life experiences, their fear and a whole myriad of other variables. My point is this: all twenty-five of the witnesses' stories may be accurate in many details yet inaccurate in others based on their perspective (view) of the scene. This is especially important to note when we are working in relationship with others (and nearly everything is about relationship with others) or working in teams. Everyone has a different perspective and no single perspective is the only right one. Being open to hearing, seeing and experiencing different perspectives is critical to expansion and forward movement individually and as a group. When we truly listen to another's perspective, we are not only honoring them, we are allowing our own expansion of perspective as well.

When clients share a concern and we delve deeper into the details of their perspective of the issue, I am aware their perspective is typically limited as they are invested in or attached to the outcome. I look for more positive perspectives with which to allow their angst over the concern to alleviate while changing absolutely nothing about the actual issue. We are simply conversing. However, offering a more positive perspective changes everything about how they see it. Their outlook improves which may then enhance their ability to accept and embrace the situation, or their desire and ability to change the situation may be enhanced. Either way, it's a win for the clients, their circle of influence and anyone in the ripple effects of their new positive perspectives.

Recently, a new client was sharing his dilemma with me in session. He had devoted many years to helping his wife's business grow and become successful. Such success had led to several larger companies vying for the opportunity to buy them out. He knew he would be unemployed soon and saw this as starting over. I offered a different perspective. He was not truly starting over. He had dozens of valuable skills and talents and career experiences. He wasn't yet forty years old either. He really wasn't starting over; he was stepping off that career path and stepping over and stepping onto another. The perspective of stepping over to another path is completely different than the perspective of starting from scratch in another career field. By offering a more positive perspective, it helped to alleviate the subconscious fear he was experiencing at the thought of literally starting over. With a new, positive perspective, he was able to embrace the idea of starting on a new and different path. He was able to see his talents and skills with a fresh mindset. He became more open to discovering what he wanted for himself at this point in the journey.

I have watched numerous clients erroneously believe they cannot change situations or circumstances that affect them. I can't tell you how many times I have heard people refer to the Serenity Prayer as a way of closing the door to their ability to influence change or make a difference for themselves or for others. I vividly remember one client, Sharon, reciting the Serenity Prayer and shrugging her shoulders after stating how she just had to get over the fact her daughter "hated" her. Wow, was she in for an exercise in the Triple P Approach. For the next thirty minutes, she attempted repeatedly to justify her desire for inaction and acceptance of the status quo. She fought hard for her inability to influence her daughter and inspire a change in the relationship. In the following ten minutes, as she examined her true intention in wanting to walk away, she discovered it was just too painful to keep trying. She had subconsciously decided it was easier and more tolerable for her to accept the situation as it were and walk away. She said, "Knowing I don't have to do anything about it and just accept it makes it easier." However, as evidenced by her emotional pain, it was not fully acceptable to her and she deeply desired a better result.

By the end of the session, Sharon had seen the situation from different perspectives and decided to give this Triple P Approach a valiant effort. After several sessions and some healing of her own emotional wounds, she felt empowered to chat with her daughter again. The desire for conversation had a ripple effect we couldn't see yet. Her intention to empower herself and her daughter with a positive perspective also had a ripple effect we couldn't predict.

We know the feeling of empowerment is profound. Think about the pleasant ripple effect of Sharon's thoughts and actions becoming more purposely positive. It starts with the relationship with her daughter and expands through both of their circles of influence and beyond. When Sharon called her daughter, she had set her intention that she speak from her heart, hear from her daughter's heart and ask for all old issues to be dissolved. Their conversation was pleasant, included laughter, and closed with a plan for the next call. What a blessing for both of them and a ripple effect of positivity far beyond their understanding.

We are never powerless

The Serenity Prayer was crafted by Reinhold Niebuhr. He is given credit for writing it as far back as the mid thirties. His original wording is a wee bit different, but the meaning remains the same. The Serenity Prayer is one of the spiritual tools used by virtually all twelve-step recovery support groups. It has also found its way into mainstream conversations and is often used as a spiritual pillar upon which to lean in troubled times. The famous interpretation reads:

God grant me the serenity to
Accept the things I cannot change,
Courage to change the things I can
And the wisdom to know the difference.

Although I honor this poem and its meaning, I am offering a different perspective to consider.

First line: "God grant me the serenity to". We all like serenity, peace and calm. Most humans do. I encourage empowerment and bravery as well as determination, fearlessness, valor and spunk. I convey to my clients, workshop attendees and now you, empowering and pleasing perspectives. We collaborate to reinforce those unrestricted outlooks and positive viewpoints. I believe having purposeful positive perspectives is attainable for all who are willing to seek them and stretch out of their rut (or current comfort zone) to discover them. I believe serenity pairs well with empowerment.

Now, let's ponder the second line: "Accept the things I cannot change." Acceptance means we approve, agree or consent. If we cannot change things, should we accept them? Meaning we approve of them, agree with them or consent to them? I'm not accepting this whole-heartedly. (Did you catch that?) I'd like to offer a different perspective.

After some deeper exploration and more investigation, we may find we *do* have the ability to change or at the very least, we have the ability to positively influence those things we thought we could never change. We may not be able to get someone else to change, but we certainly can improve our relationship with him or her. We can alter or shift our part of any relationship, and pretty much anything with anyone is relationship.

When we purposefully positively improve our part of any relationship the other is influenced in a positive way also. Our perspective improves, the energy of the relationship transforms, and the other in the relationship is positively influenced. When we hold the intention of an improved, healthy relationship, we focus on the improvements and they seem to magically appear. The other may not have consciously chosen to work towards improving the relationship, but he or she will certainly be reaping the benefits of the positive influence. This usually leads towards an overall healthier relationship and often leads to a healing of the relationship for both parties.

Sometimes the conflict just dissolves without further work to resolve it. Remember that this applies to any type of relationship whether it is seen as equal (friend, sibling, or colleague) or within an accepted hierarchy (boss, subordinate, authority figure). The type of relationship does not matter to the outcome of this positive influence. Thus, I always encourage a more purposeful positive exploration with a proactive movement. To positively influence a situation, be proactive and purposeful rather than allowing yourself passive acceptance.

Some have argued that we cannot change the past. Although I agree we cannot change the facts of history, we can certainly change, shift and improve how we feel about them. We can, with our intention and the Triple P Approach, transform our emotional connection to the past. That, my friends, is immeasurable in helping us to move forward, to heal emotional traumas, and to improve the trajectory of our future. When considering "things I cannot change", I will always offer up a Triple P because I am certain we are never powerless. I believe we always have the power of purposeful, positive perspectives and we always have the purposeful power of prayer. Remember, our words are prayer. When we choose a positive perspective, we upgrade the thoughts, energy and emotions connected to the event as well.

In a recent survey, I asked hundreds of people what they believe they cannot change. As you might expect, there were a few comments about the weather, taxes, and natural disasters. Several people responded that we are unable to change death. Many people responded with statements about being unable to change others' opinions, actions, behaviors, feelings, and choices. Several responses were related to family and our inability to change who they are and what they do. There were comments about being unable to change the past, our childhood, and the choices of our parents or other adults in our past, which directly or indirectly affected us. Several comments delved deeper into the inability to change past decisions or actions. And there were multiple comments about not being able to change our destiny, our life purpose or who we were meant to be. Some responses were sassy and others were intriguing.

I read each response carefully and thoughtfully. Several of the responses left me pondering for quite some time. The majority of the responses were well-worded and thought-provoking. For each response I received, I began processing a purposeful positive perspective. Using the Triple P concept changes our view of the event, which has a profound affect upon our feelings about the event. We cannot change the actual event, but by looking at it from a more positive perspective, we can change the emotions and energy attached to it. The ripple effect that follows from this shift in thinking is of unknown proportions and unlimited potential.

As I stated earlier, we have the power to positively impact and improve relationships regardless of others' input or intention to do the same. Every human has free will. Because of free will, even a Guardian Angel cannot interfere with a human and his or her free will choices. Although we cannot directly change another's behaviors or choices, we certainly can and we do influence him or her with our choices and behaviors. And we impact him or her with our thoughts and our energy when around them. Thus, if we are in alignment with our positive perspectives, we positively affect everyone around us, including family, friends, neighbors and coworkers. The positive influence impressed upon them changes them even if only a small percentage.

Notice, I have not included much discussion about the power of prayer even though there are many studies which prove the capacity prayer has in positively influencing the health and healing of our self and others. For example, when we are actively praying for another family member to have resolution from past incidents or events, the person being prayed for is positively affected and thus changed for the better. When we are praying for someone's current situation to improve for their best and highest potential, we are improving the energy around them and positively enhancing them as well.

We are never powerless. We always have the power of intention and the power of prayer. Regardless of religion, spiritual depth or the verbiage we use to pray, the power of prayer makes a purposeful and positive difference for the person, family or situation for which prayer is being offered. Our words are prayer. Our thoughts are prayer too. Words spoken, written, or thought are prayer. It's not about the space we're in or the way we do it as much as it is about our intention. Thus, a Triple P (a purposeful positive perspective) is always prayer.

I believe we are never powerless to positively influence anything and everything. Regardless if the event is past, present or anticipated in the future, we have the power to positively influence any situation and the outcome of it.

Change is a verb and is defined as follows, "to make the form, nature, content, future course, etc., of (something) different from what it is or from what it would be if left alone." Let that settle in and integrate for a moment. Read the sentence again... We know we can change our opinion, our direction, our looks, our thoughts, our feelings, our name, and so on. Anything we can control, we can change. Now... let's explore how we can make the form, nature, or future course of something in our past different from what it is or what it would be if left alone. What?

Too many people believe we cannot change anything about the past. They also believe those are the very things we need to "accept that we cannot change." I believe it is appropriate to explore our ability to affect the future course of those past events and how they relate to our present and our future. Changing our perspective of them means altering our viewpoint and our attitude towards them. When we transform our thinking and emotions toward past events we allow a metamorphosis to occur. We release the barriers to our spiritual growth and we soar to new heights of happiness.

It may be helpful to bring a few sensitive topics into this discussion which will bring insight and may be quite healing for many readers. Statistically speaking, child abuse or neglect in some form has been in the life experience of more than half of the population. Survivors will most certainly agree the abuse occurred and that fact cannot be changed. By embracing the Serenity Prayer, we are asked to accept the abuse and accept that we cannot change it. As stated earlier, accepting means to approve, agree or consent. I have been teaching about recognizing and preventing child abuse since 2004. There have been thousands of participants in those classes. I do not see acceptance in the faces of those who have been abused. Instead, survivors of child abuse often mask the pain with drugs or alcohol. They may perpetrate the abuse on others. They may have such anger or hurt that they are chronically depressed, extremely introverted, guarded or withdrawn. They may be so angry they seldom see or experience joy or happiness in their life experiences. They may spend the remainder of their life trying to figure out why this happened to them or why they "deserved" it. They often struggle through life trying to find their true nature and wanting to heal their wounded inner-child. A relatively small number of abuse survivors will use the experience to stop the violence within the family or turn it around to help others. In any case, there is seldom approval or acceptance of what happened.

Can we change the events as they occurred? No. However we can, "make the form, nature, content, future course, etc., of (something) different from what it is or from what it would be if left alone". Ahhhh… now do you see it? As we begin the process of seeking purposeful positive perspectives, we also begin the healing process. When we improve our perspective we improve our outlook. As our outlook improves, everything improves! Our thoughts become more positive and our energy rises. And the ripple effect continues to positively influence our relationships and beyond. Therefore, because we can "make the form, nature, content, or future course" different, we *can change* it. We cannot change the events as they occurred. Left alone, the emotions connected to those events can wreak havoc with our health and our life circumstances. With a new, positive perspective, we change the entire future course! Embrace that wisdom and understanding!

Available statistics from varying data bases indicate a significant majority of the population has been the victim of some sort of violent or serious crime. For each of us, the facts of the event (or events) cannot be changed. As stated in the previous discussion regarding abuse, we know we are changed by that violence. Some would argue we are damaged by it. We can choose to live our life with the perspective of being the victim or being damaged. We can choose to let the violence and its outcome define us and our future. We can also choose to move forward with as much grace and dignity as we can by seeking a proactive and positive perspective about our past, present and future.

Which do you prefer: Remain angry, hurt, damaged, victimized, disempowered and stuck in the energy of it, or bring in the energy of strength, courage, healing and empower yourself to live the rest of your life with positive perspectives? It's your choice. You have free will. My wish for you, is that you will harness the power of positive perspectives and embrace the freedom that comes when allowing the past to be healed.

This is where the next line of the Serenity Prayer becomes helpful. It reads, "Courage to change the things I can". When we recognize the possibility of being able to positively influence and change nearly everything in our life, we must also have the courage to do so.

Many people believe there is nothing they can do to influence change in events, situations, or experiences. It may be deeply imprinted in their belief system. It may be a part of their subconscious programming from childhood. They may be afraid of moving forward or have a fear of success. They may have become comfortable in their discomfort. They know the discomfort. For so many, as awful as the uncomfortable situation is, at least they know it. They can navigate their way through it.

Courage is the ability to take steps forward, without fear. Fear of the unknown keeps many people immobile. For others, it is the fear of what life will be like without this known pain, hurt or anger that keeps them stuck. When they are empowered with the knowledge and awareness that they can positively affect change, it opens up Pandora's Box. It is a box of unbridled fear or it's a pathway of unlimited opportunity. This awareness alone can be frightening. However, awareness, coupled with the desire to make the change, empowers us to make it happen.

Empowerment means to give it power. Feeling empowered to make change drives us to go forth. Everyone who has the awareness and the desire will do well when supported and encouraged. Being supported while making change will be helpful but it is not necessary when we have our own inner strength and courage driving us forward. True courage comes from within. It is about trusting in the process and allowing it to unfold as we provide the positive intention and energy for it. There is nothing to fear. When we keep the focus on positive perspectives, we keep the process moving forward in positive ways. There is more to fear in staying stuck and stationary- the status quo. We already know that isn't working in our best interest or it wouldn't be so dissatisfying and uncomfortable.

This purposeful process is driven from within. Again, it starts with your thoughts, your desires and your focused attention. You move forward with or without outside support. You empower yourself with your own decisions, actions, reactions and thoughts. And your courage is fueled by your desire for positive outcome. It's about you and it's for you.

The final line in the Serenity Prayer reads, "And wisdom to know the difference". Wisdom is defined as: "knowledge of what is true or right, coupled with just judgment as to action." It's about discernment and insight, and for some, it's as simple as common sense. After reading, engaging with and embracing the information in this chapter, you will easily develop the discernment and the wisdom for your greatest and highest potential. You will find your inner strength and courage to make improvements and affect change. You will seldom feel powerless again. You will remember how you always have the power of prayer and positive intention. You will seek more opportunities to be proactive and purposeful. You will help to educate and guide others to also seek purposeful positive perspectives. The ripple effect will be extraordinary!

Chapter 7
The Ripple Effect
It Starts with You

For everything, there is a ripple effect. A stone tossed into a body of water creates an ever expanding ripple that continues across the entire surface all the way to the edges. Every movement causes a shift of air flow and energy that ripples out into the atmosphere. Every sound is a vibration that ripples out, endlessly, into the universe. Regardless of whether those sound vibrations are heard or not, the vibration ripples on and on.

The Ripple Effect is defined as: the gradual spreading effect of influence; the repercussions of an event far beyond its immediate location; a series of consequences caused by a single event or action.

Every action, every reaction, every decision and every thought causes a ripple effect that continues indefinitely. We typically lack awareness of this ripple and its outcome. That lack of awareness on our part does not change the fact that the ripples occur and continue. People are affected, situations transform, vibrations shift, emotions are stirred, events are influenced. Then, as physics would have it, each ripple allows for change and each change initiates yet another ripple effect. The cycles go on and on in ever increasing and never ending succession.

You can study the scientific explanation of The Ripple Effect and you will have an understanding of the principles, but the ripple effect of our own thoughts, actions, reactions, and decisions are far more complicated to understand. When we develop an understanding of or, at the very least, have an interest in understanding the ripple effect of our behaviors, we immediately have the opportunity to change the trajectory of our life. As we learn how the ripple effect of what we do, say, and think affects our world, and as we begin to focus purposely, proactively and positively, we initiate a transformation! It happens first within us.

It starts within each of us individually. It starts with you. It starts with me. We initiate the ripples of change within our own life. You initiate the ripples of change within your family. You initiate the ripples of change within your community. You may have felt you were just one person and couldn't possibly have such a profound effect. You may have thought you have no ability to affect positive change or initiate such a transformation all by yourself. In truth, yes you can. And, YES you do.

Whether you know it consciously or not, you are influencing your present, your future, your family, your workplace, your community and the world with every thought and every action or reaction you choose. That prospect can be very scary and overwhelming OR it can be incredibly empowering. It is totally up to you which perspective you choose. I hope you will consider how empowering it truly is to be in a position to know you can positively influence anything and everything in the world with just your thoughts and actions. When disempowering thoughts prevail, we can change them quickly and easily. And with that modification in thought comes a transformation in energy vibration and that, my friend, is empowering! This begins the ripple effect.

The ripple effect of our purposeful positive perspective improvements are like the undulations which ripple across the surface of the pond. The magnitude of those undulations is the greatest at the initiation point, meaning that the biggest changes occur at the point of origin. We are the initiation point, so the biggest and most transformative changes occur within and around us. The initiation point becomes the center of focus from which the undulations (or waves of intention) begin to form and flow outward in a never ending and consistent pattern of concentric circles.

It is the energy in those undulations emanating from the center that have the power to influence everything in its path. Visualize a pebble being tossed into a pond. Where the pebble enters the water becomes the center point of the undulations that we will call the waves of change. The size of those initial undulations (waves) is at their greatest size closest to the initiation point. We watch as the undulations caused by the pebble slowly ripple outward touching everything in its path.

It is the same with the ripple effect of our actions, reactions, thoughts, decisions or anything that initiates with us. We create the shift with our actions or thoughts and that shift become the point of origin or the initiation point. The undulations, those waves of change, that start the ripple effect, begin with us. The energy in those undulations emanate from us. It is the energy of our action, reaction, or thought which emanates outward in the flow of energy influencing and affecting everything in its path.

There is great wisdom in Mahatma Gandhi's words, "You must BE the change you wish to see in the world." This quote is from decades ago. He knew long ago that all change begins with a single thought from a single being. Therefore, we should never feel small or powerless. We should never feel as if we cannot impact or influence an improvement in something within our own life or countries away. We can! (And I'm trying to imprint this concept for you in every way I can write it.)

I must also include here that this concept is universal. It happens whether we know it or not. It happens whether it is purposeful or not. It happens whether it is positive or not. Without purposeful and proactive intent, we can get caught up in the ripple effect of someone else's thoughts and emotions. It happens to us more often than we realize. Someone tells us their tale of woe we are sad for the rest of the day. Someone near us is experiencing extreme anxiety and soon we are anxious without understanding why.

Now that we are armed with the understanding of how energy follows thought, we know that when we create a shift of energy within us the vibration of the shift emanates outward in all directions. When we are feeling joy, we are emanating the vibration of joy in an unceasing cascade which affects everyone and everything in its path. Similarly, when we are feeling angry, we are emanating the vibration of anger in an unceasing cascade which affects everyone and everything in its path.

Thinking thoughts of love, joy, peace, contentment, and appreciation raise the vibration of our energy, our spirit and of our being. Keep in mind, the energy vibration we are holding within us is also the energy vibration we are radiating. It is rippling out from us like a tidal wave. We are affecting everything around us with our vibration thus we are either raising the vibration around us or lowering it. We are either paying attention to our intention or we are ignoring it. We are either providing a positive perspective improvement or a negative one. We are either being purposefully positive or we are not. We are either seeking an improved perspective or we are not. It's one or the other. There is no true neutral because if we are not being intentional we are being the pinball. So we are either moving with purpose or moving by Universal pinball paddles.

When we are not purposely positive, we inadvertently lower our vibration. Whether it is intentional, accidental or subconscious, the outcome is the same. It's like turning off an electric fan. The blades are able to move with the flow of air around it but the ability to influence the air flow of the room is gone. It is instead being influenced by its surroundings.

This is a good time to talk physics and science for a moment. **Energy** – All matter has energy. It cannot be created or destroyed but can be used, moved and influenced. Energy is measurable. Food energy is measured in calories. We measure heat energy in temperature. A joule is a measure of work energy. Wattage is a measure of electrical energy, and so on. **Vibration** – is created when something moves. Pluck a harp string and the vibration creates the sound we hear. **Frequency** - the number of times something (harp string) vibrates. Although we cannot see the number of times (frequency) the string vibrates, there are instruments that measure the frequency of vibrating objects.

Humans have energy. We have measurable vibration because parts of our body are in constant motion. Our heart is pumping our blood throughout our entire bloodstream, organs and tissues. Our innards are always working thus there is continual motion (vibration) within our being. Because there is continual motion we have a measurable frequency. This frequency can be measured up to several feet away from the human body. This measurable area around the human body is known as the energy field. Scientists have been studying the energy field around humans and or human body parts since the early sixties. We know, scientifically, our thoughts affect our energy vibration which is measured as the frequency changes. The science of it is fascinating!

When we purposely work to improve our thinking, we raise our vibrational frequency which in turn improves the health and wellness of our body. When our energy vibration lowers, so does the vibration of the energy in our body and all around us. Do you see how our thinking influences our health and well-being?

If we live or work in an environment that we consider toxic or negative, it will take purposeful, proactive attention, intention and action to influence and improve the energy vibration around us. Unfortunately, most people who work in this type of environment give up and succumb to the lower vibrational ripples. They are negatively influenced and affected by the toxic tide and soon they may be so profoundly affected it impacts other areas of their life, too. It's hard work to be the bright ray of sunshine in an environment overcast with gloom. (The stronger energy wins!) Radiating the Triple P's is the best approach but not always the easiest. It takes an intentional effort to remain unattached to the outcome of others' events and life situations. It also requires a stronger vibration to overcome the vibration of negativity. It may not be easy but it is definitely worth the effort.

I often use the following analogy when I am teaching about the raising and lowering of vibrations: Consider how we heat water for tea. We turn on the burner and eventually the water heats up. As long as the water temperature is climbing, the vibration is raising. When we turn the temperature down or off, the water cools and the vibrations will lower. We can, with a flip of a dial, raise and lower the temperature, (vibrations). It is much the same with us. We can, with a flip of a thought or action, raise or lower the vibrations of our energy. We can also allow ourselves to be influenced by the energy vibration of someone else. It's our choice. When we are clear about our intention, purposeful with our thoughts and actions, we choose to be the keeper of our own energy field and its vibrational frequency.

Think about someone you may know who is always complaining about something. Nothing ever works out well for them…life is difficult… they struggle…. And so on… No one enjoys being around someone like this. Often we will hear people describe these souls as "draining" or as "energy vampires". They most certainly are draining. My friend says, "They suck the life right out of you!" Unless you are able to keep your vibration high, the ripple effect of their lower energy vibration is likely to influence and lower yours. Frankly, it is easier to drop to their lower level vibration than it is to bring them up to yours. Our higher vibration must be the stronger vibration in order to positively affect theirs. To keep our energy vibration up, we keep our positive perspective. To keep our energy vibration strong, we are purposeful and use our intention.

Let's talk physics again. What I just described are the principles of resonance and entrainment in action. **Resonance** – when one vibrating object causes another object to vibrate at the same or similar frequency. **Entrainment** – when two vibrating objects are in proximity, the object with the weaker vibration will entrain to the object with the stronger vibration.

When discussing musical instruments or pendulum clocks, this makes perfect sense. How do we apply these principles to humans? Remember the human body is in constant motion creating continual vibrations that have measurable frequency. Therefore, our energy field emits or radiates a vibrational frequency. When we work closely with someone, our energy fields are in proximity. (We vibrate – they vibrate.) If the stronger vibration of the two energy fields is pleasant and positive (higher vibration), the other will entrain (rise up) to it. If the stronger vibration is angry, pessimistic or depressed (lower vibration), the other will entrain (lower) to it. We simply assure our energy vibration is higher and stronger.

From reading about the Triple P's in this book you already know how to keep your energy vibration high. To assure our energy vibration is strong, we use our intention and power it up with the emotions that match. Keeping a positive perspective keeps our vibrational frequency high which helps to keep our body healthy. A healthy body has a hardy vibration. A hardy, robust vibration is a strong vibration. Are you getting this? Healthy thoughts = healthy body. Healthy body = healthy thoughts. Healthy thoughts + healthy body = happy life. It is all connected and literally driven by our own thoughts/thinking. Think about that!

Surprisingly, many people do not want to make the effort for improved life circumstances. The reasons vary. Frequently they are unable to visualize or understand the ripple effect of a purposely positive experience. However, knowing what you know now, you can choose to keep your thinking in a positive perspective and hold your energy vibration strong. This means you will not be as likely to be drained by those types of individuals. The more awareness you have and the more you practice purposeful positive perspectives, the more your own inner strength will prevail. Ultimately, it means the ripple effect of your stronger high vibration affects the whiner/complainer. Soon, a shift will occur. They will either choose not to be around you (for whatever reason they perceive) OR they will feel shifted for the better every time they are around you, feeling the ripple effect of being in your presence. Either result is a win!

Think about someone you may know, or wish to know, who is happy, carefree, or has other attributes which you find appealing. You enjoy being around this person and they seem to lift you up. These are the best people to surround yourself as they help you raise or maintain your own energy vibration. Being surrounded by those with a higher vibration than yours helps you to raise your vibration, allowing you to emanate and radiate a higher vibration to others. We become active participants in this higher vibration and the ripple effect is incredible. This is how grassroots movements gain momentum to resolve community issues.

If we sit back and do nothing but absorb while in this space, we become the energy drain. Think about that the next time you are in a place that truly lifts your spirits high. Do you entrain to that frequency and then share that energy with others or do you revel in it for a while and then move on. Do you strengthen the ripple effect or do you provide a ripple roadblock?

In order to fully understand the ripple effect as it relates to energy, thoughts, and actions, we have to look at the big picture, too.

Yes, we know every change begins with us and the ripples emanate from us. But what happens in the family or the workplace? What happens in community? What happens when thousands of people have the same or similar thoughts, fears, energy vibration or actions and behaviors? Here are just a few examples of how the ripple effect works in our reality.

In Chapter 2, I described an exercise I experienced in nursing school. Now I will explain in more detail how we performed this experiment. Our instructor, Ms. Lind, asked a student, I'll call her Susan, who agreed to be the test subject. Susan left the room so as not to hear the instructions. We were given two tasks. When Ms. Lind said "Go", we were to focus our thoughts on mean things and think of Susan as weak. We were to hold those nasty thoughts for one full minute then Ms. Lind would muscle test the student's strength. Next, Ms. Lind would tell us to switch and we were to hold loving thoughts and think of Susan as strong. Ms. Lind would again test the student's strength. Susan was called back into the classroom. The teacher told her to just stand there and relax for a minute. Ms. Lind told us "Go". For the full minute we focused our thoughts on negative things. After the minute, Ms. Lind asked us to stop and asked the student to hold out her arm. Ms. Lind told the student to keep it strong while she tried to push Susan's arm down. It went down so quickly it surprised Susan as well as the rest of us. Then, Ms. Lind said "switch". We held loving, helpful thoughts and thought of Susan as strong for a full minute. Ms. Lind then retested Susan. We all were shocked to see that Susan held her arm strong no matter what the amount of pressure Ms. Lind applied. This experiment was a life altering moment for me. It probably was for other students as well. I found it fascinating that the focused attention on our intention influenced and affected Susan so easily, so quickly and so profoundly. As I mentioned earlier, I knew I needed to make changes for myself and my family. But I also realized the power of many when thinking or acting in collaboration!

Here is another personal experience: Several years ago I was the General Manager of a home care and hospice branch of a large, national company. Our branch was rather small with only about seventy employees. Several members of my management team were happy, thoughtful, considerate and generally fun to be around. Two managers gave the appearance of being happy yet consistently found fault with others and frequently gossiped and made fun of those staff members who were the rays of sunshine. It was a challenge to manage those two because their energy was very strong. The ripple effect of their toxic tide was pervasive and soon it became a disciplinary issue. Up to a point, I was able to maintain the high level of resonance and energy frequency necessary to keep our workplace pleasant and enjoyable. However, when I was out of the office for a week of vacation, those two managers created a toxic tsunami so strong the other staff members could not fight it.

When I returned, the energy in the office was sullen, fearful, and caustic. The ripple effect of their negativity was palpable. Behind closed doors, staff members told me what had happened in my absence. Energetically, it was fascinating! Those two resonated with such disdain for happiness; the ripple effect they created was to dissolve anything that resembled happy, joyful, or pleasant. They replaced the positive attributes with negativity and fear. They believed it gave them power. Unfortunately, at some level it did. They became emboldened and empowered. It amazed me how easy it was for those generally happy staff members to succumb to the lower vibration. It had become too powerful to override it. Thankfully, it was also easy to restore them to their generally happy dispositions once the toxic tide was stopped and the ripples of negativity had been road-blocked. Those two managers lost their jobs that week. Sadly, they chose a purposely negative perspective. The ripple effect was huge! They lost their jobs which affected their families, which caused…. on and on and on those ripples surged.

On a happier note, I remember having an engaging conversation with several women who work in a school. I thought they were all teachers. One woman corrected me by saying, "I'm just the lunch lady." Turns out she is the cashier at the junior high. As I looked at her, I was awed by the energy around her. She was literally angelic! She radiated a high vibration. She was delightful, happy and smiled non-stop. I shared with her the philosophy of the ripple effect of purposeful positive perspectives and how just a smile can change the energy for another. I knew she was different; she knew what I was talking about. She didn't use the same words and said she didn't really understand mine. However, her Spirit knew exactly what she was doing and why! As we talked, she shared how she made a point to look each child in the eye and tell them something special she noticed about them. She made sure to touch them when she gave them change or had them sign for their lunch. She knew which children needed the little extras she doled out and which children were hurt so deeply she hadn't gotten through yet. Yes, she knew what role she played on this planet. She knew her life purpose was much bigger and far more important than the job she held to perform her mission.

That conversation was validation that this theory, the Ripple Effect, was more powerful than even I imagined. Following the ripple effect of her positive perspective with those children would be a daunting task. There are hundreds of children influenced daily by her positive perspective and each of them creates ripples too.

Recently, a new client came to see me. She wanted career coaching. She is a Human Relations Director in a relatively large firm. She was beginning to feel that her job/career were not enough. She felt that maybe there was something else out there she was "supposed to be doing" and she was afraid she was missing it. I asked her very important questions and probed to learn more about her core values and what made her heart happy. As we chatted, I remembered the lunch lady. Instantly my mind was flooded with visions of this HR manager guiding people and helping them navigate career changes, disciplinary issues, corporate programs, etc. By the end of the session, she knew she was right where she was "supposed to be". She was doing what makes her heart sing. She is making a positive impact every day.

Two big waves were started with that session. The ripple effect with her career was immediately felt as she realigned with her vision and core values and reengaged with her role. The other big wave rippled across her immediate and her extended family and then her faith community. She found her purpose again and realized her value. She stepped into her career role and validated her self value which allowed her to emanate confidence and happiness. That wave allowed for ripples of contentment and peace. As our purposeful, positive perspective becomes stronger and more intentional, the ripple effect lifts our family in such a way the ripples never cease.

The opposite is also true. When we have a pervasive pool of pessimistic thinkers or aggressive, adverse actions by a group of contrary citizens, the ripple effect can be palpable. When a considerable number of beings are sending out ripples, those ripples can be felt physically, emotionally and spiritually. They create somewhat of a huge wave like those the surfers love, maybe a Maverick or a Pipeline. Surfers love these huge magnificent waves. Yet, like the Maverick or Pipeline, the sheer size and magnitude of these waves can be deadly. I'm talking about waves of energy caused by a large group of people.

The wave of energy, the ripples of intention, takes on the energy of those who created it. If they are happy and excited (New Year's Eve in Times Square), the energy resonates with happiness and enthusiasm. Remember, intention means everything. Large groups of people coming together in prayer or for the healing of a community such as those experienced after natural disasters are heroic in nature and have huge healing benefits for all. That is the intention and all thoughts are for helpful healing. Energy follows the thoughts and great things happen. The ripple effect can be felt for days, weeks, and years into the future. Individual ripple effects may spark a career choice in a young teenager or introduce a deeper compassion in an adult who was feeling lost. There is no end to these ripples of purposeful, positive energies.

However, if those in the group are angry, hostile, or frustrated, the resulting "mob mentality" often turns to vandalism and violence, rioting and looting. The energy frequency of the group attracts more of those who are angry and frustrated. And the ripple effect of such hostility is as huge and dangerous as the Maverick wave formations. The intention of the group is to express their outrage. There is little or no accountability for individual actions or behaviors because they grumble how they "got caught up in it." The intention is nothing helpful or proactive and everyone has lost his or her positive perspective.

The ripple effects of these events go far beyond our ability to track. Each individual has his or her own ripple effect. The event may have caused such anger as to spark an illness within an individual. A family may become divided. The community, the region, the country, and the world all have ripple effects far beyond our ability to see and understand.

My first experience witnessing a large angry group (mob mentality) was the Los Angeles riots in the early ninety's. The ripple effect was tremendous. It continues yet today. With a bit of effort to pay attention to our intention, these events would diminish rapidly. More importantly, it is those who are witnessing or watching from afar who can impact the situation by sending love, peace and understanding to the area rather than focusing on fear and irritation. By sending positive energies we can literally diffuse those types of events quicker than the National Guard!

Fear is another emotion with unfavorable energetic ripples. The most tremendous ripple effect I've ever witnessed was September 11, 2001. The worldwide fear felt on 9/11 had the most profound effect on many levels. And the ripple effect continues yet today! Many different types of ripple effects emanated from the 9/11 terrorist attacks. Fear is just one of them.

Fear blocks our ability to adequately reason and process. It takes a serious and concentrated effort to refocus and find a positive perspective if we are trying to save our life or the lives of others. Again, it is those who are witnessing the event from afar who have the ability to provide the greatest influence and impact.

A frenzy initiated by Black Friday sales has caused a type of mob mentality culminating in stampedes that resulted in serious injuries and death as well as property damage. The intention of origin? To secure a sale item? Those with Triple P will sense the energy shifting and will step back from the situation or will try to diffuse it. Remember, we are never powerless. We always have the power of our intention, our energy vibration and our thoughts to influence the outcome to a more positive and peaceful resolution.

What about global actions? I'm speaking about the *fights against* cancer, drugs, terrorism, violence, and war. Think about the energy of fighting a fight. Think about the ripple effect of that energy emanating outward: the anger, the hostility, the fight. Does it really matter what the fight is about when the energy is still about fighting? NO! We can not now nor can we ever win a fight against or a fight for anything. Because in the energy of fighting or protesting or demanding, we are emanating the energy and emotion of negativity and the ripples continue on and on - as does the originating issue. In all the years of fighting the fights, have we defeated the drug trade? Have we ended war? Have we conquered cancer? Have we thwarted terrorism? Are we winning?

When we are truly ready, we will take on the purposeful positive perspective and BE the change we are wishing to see in the world. To stop violence and war, we must promote and cause ripples of peace and harmony. To stop the drug trade, we must promote health, wellness, hope and peace of mind. Happy people do not want to fight and will find ways to radiate happiness. Happy people do not seek an escape into drugs and drug trafficking. Happy people promote happiness, spread peace and seek joy. Positive perspectives allay fears. Promoting health and wellness prevents disease and illness. Promote peace and peace will reign. Peace comes in many forms. Promoting peace of mind eliminates depression, anxiety and fear. Envision this!

Do you understand how we can choose a positive perspective and everything, I mean everything, changes? (I really had to think and re-think about this to actually get it and embrace it.) But when you do, when you really get it and engage with it and practice choosing a purposeful positive perspective, it will change your life! When you intentionally transform your thinking, your life will transform. The level of the transformation will be directly proportional to the level of positive perspectives you choose. The level of transformation will be the direct outcome of your intention.

Science shows us how consistently moving wind or water can alter landscape and terrain. That same moving wind or water can, over time, cause incredible erosion, resulting in amazingly beautiful creations or destroying an entire geography. The wind can create natural arches made within huge rock formations. Ocean waves repeatedly pounding into cliffs made of rock can create beautiful natural sculptures which cannot be duplicated by man.

Conversely, flowing rivers can wreak havoc when the natural flow is constricted or redirected. Consistent action and/or movement impacts and influences change. The ripple effect of these types of changes are also far reaching and never ceasing. They can be positive and beautiful or they can be damaging and harmful.

Consider the ripple effect of a river whose flow is redirected by man. The change to the landscape and geography are immediate. However, the ripple effect continues throughout nature. The natural habitat of the area is impacted which causes changes for the fish and other water animals, the birds, and the animals who use this water for their needs. We have learned over the course of many years that the environmental impact of man's interference with nature causes far reaching ripple effects. Armed with this understanding, we now require environmental impact studies prior to making shifts in the natural land or water pathways.

Because the ripple effect of each and every action is far reaching, we do well for ourselves and others when we consider how the ripple effect of our actions and decisions will affect us and others around us. It is very similar to performing our own personal environmental impact study. It's the pause we take before speaking. It's the breath we take before acting. Both actions give us just a moment to ask ourselves about our true intention. By paying attention to our intention and consistently engaging with purposeful, positive perspectives, we radiate a ripple effect of beautiful potential and positivity that never ceases.

Chapter 8
You have the Power
Use it Wisely

WHAT YOU EXPECT YOU ACCEPT! When you expect that something will occur, you have already accepted it into your reality. Pay attention to your intention. Then, expect all good things. Make way for good happenings in your life. Keep your thoughts focused on good things. Seek good vibrations!

Are our thoughts really that powerful, you ask? Yes, they are really that powerful. Studies on neuroscience, epigenetics, and quantum physics continue to prove the power of our thoughts, intention and energy. It's not just my opinion or my philosophy. It's scientific fact.

While gardening today, I was pondering how the seeds fall from the trees and immediately begin the process to become new trees. It doesn't matter if the seed falls in a gutter, a crack in the sidewalk, or in a wet pile of leaves. The seeds begin to grow. There is no question what they will become. The seed does not doubt itself. They are programmed by higher intelligence to become trees. The same occurs for all plants and their seeds. It's somewhat true for animals.

However, in addition to their higher intelligence programming (instinct), animals have some options for making choices.

I recently watched a video of a cat who, in the first hours after giving birth to her litter of kittens, had also adopted newly hatched ducklings. She mothered them like her kittens and the ducklings enjoyed the warmth of their newfound family. However, the ducklings soon grew into mature ducks while the kittens matured into cats. Their genetic programming included feathers for the ducks and fur for the felines. Kittens meow and ducks quack. No matter the nurture, nature prevails.

Plants and animals are hard wired to their genetics. They need no intervention to fulfill their destiny. They will become exactly what they are genetically programmed to be. Plants are nurtured by warmth, sunlight and water. Although many studies have proven the positive affects pleasant music and affection have on plants, it is not required for their growth. Mammals are nurtured by warmth, sunlight, water and nutrition as well. However, without affection and the positive energy vibration affection brings, growth may be slowed and result in Failure to Thrive (FTT).

Those who work with plants and animals share some amazing stories. Animals, once thought to have no emotions, have been recorded clearly showing emotions from happiness to grief and sorrow. Animals, once thought to have no ability to comprehend have been recorded completing complex tasks to attain a goal. Animals, once thought unable to communicate, have been recorded communicating with others in their own family groupings as well as with other species.

Studies are well documented that demonstrate how plants are affected by different environments (hostile or happy) and different music (heavy metal or classical). It all relates to energy, vibration and frequency. Thoughts are emotion. Emotion is energy. We feel and respond to energy. Plants and animals feel and respond to energy. Literally everything is vibration and energy.

Many experiments have been done to demonstrate the importance of how intention and energy flow from one human towards another human influences them. Experiments have also been conducted on water, plants, rice, animals, weather and even blood and tissue samples. Fascinating studies have been conducted to follow patients who were being prayed for (positive energy) by groups or individuals from all over the world. My favorite studies about the power of prayer are those where the recipient is unaware of the influx of positive energy (prayer), and who then have quicker recovery times or experience medical miracles.

I participated with a dozen energy workers to diffuse or lessen a hurricane which was headed directly for an area of the gulf where my son was located. It was a category four when we started working. It was expected to continue to gain wind speed and reach category five by morning. We began sending love energy (or praying) with the intention to calm the storm and reduce the damage to land and people. When the hurricane made landfall, it had lessened to a category three. Once over land, it quickly dissipated. As we expected, there was minimal flooding and other hurricane related damage was also minimal. That's the power we have in groups and community! The twelve of us were very focused with our intention and expectation. I wondered how many others had the same. Our combined vibrational energy was strong enough to make a huge impact. And it was free! (Bonus!)

Incredible photographs were created to show how water is affected by prayer, rock music, classical music or simply the vibration of a written word. Dr. Emoto's life work has been well documented. His books tell an amazing journey through photographs that depict the difference made to the same water treated differently with intention. The experiments and the photographs send a very important message to each of us to raise our vibration to love, gratitude, appreciation and respect, (each of these positive emotions resulted in beautiful crystals) and to radiate that energy out to others. It makes an impressive difference. The experiments and resulting photographs were enough validation for me to pay more attention to my intention and verbiage.

One of my favorite sets of photographs Dr. Emoto published, was the before and after of a small lake which was rippled by the breeze but calmed to complete stillness after a priest prayed over it for just one minute. A simple prayer by a human was that powerful! We are that powerful! And together we are powerful beyond measure!

Human beings are in a perfect place on the planet. We have the ability to have deeper understandings of our actions and intentions. We can reason, comprehend, and communicate well. More importantly, we have the ability to influence events and happenings far behind our physical reach and far beyond our awareness and understanding. My goal with this book is to share that wisdom and facilitate the understanding so each of us joins together to positively influence our communities, countries, and the planet Earth. Just imagine ...

Chapter 9
Putting it all Together
Practice, Practice, Practice

EVERY SITUATION IS UNIQUE AND each one is affected by different circumstances. I have discovered a few types of events or situations common enough to provide as examples that may help you as you practice harnessing your power to purposely create positive perspectives. Remember these three steps:

1. Determine the Purpose
2. Set your Intention
3. Take Action

After you have determined the nature of the task or purpose, then, set your intention for the desired outcome. What do you want to occur? What do you really want? If you don't know what you want to happen as a result of your task or action, ponder and process until you do. When you step into a situation without purposeful intent for the desired outcome, you will be playing pinball and YOU will be the little silver ball.

With your intention set for desired result, you are ready to take action. Do it. Make the call - attend the meeting – perform the task. Being mindful of your intention, keep your positive perspective and your excited expectation that it WILL go as desired!

———⁎⁎⁎———

Important phone call:

Determine the purpose for the call then think about the outcome you desire. Once you are clear on what the purpose or intention is for your phone call, then you can think about what is needed to achieve the outcome you want. Do you want to resolve a difficult situation? Are you offering a solution for something? Would you like the listener to hear you with clarity? Are you hoping for a win-win consensus for something? Whatever your desired outcome, set your intention for how you'd like to accomplish it. Then, believe it. Expect it will be so. Embrace it. And make the call. You may need to write down the desired outcome to look at while you are on the call. Never lose sight of the end goal. Losing perspective may mean losing self discipline, too.

If your goal is to vent, be heard, express your outrage or something similar, I recommend you re-think your objective and wait a few days. Seldom is it helpful or productive to vent your irritation or outrage without an intentional goal or objective. Most often it creates more conflict and trauma to yourself and the recipient. There is no positive perspective present and there is nothing proactive driving towards a resolution. Furthermore, the ripple effect of the venting may be difficult to overcome or may be irreversible. The listener cannot simply "un-hear" it.

———⁎⁎⁎———

Taking an Important Test:

Start this intention-setting process early! Waiting until the night before the big test gives you little time to put much energy, effort and attention forth toward your ultimate goal. And, I'd have to question your true intention in waiting until the last minute. I also recommend setting your intention for something higher and better than "just passing". However, it is your process so you choose.

Set your intention for the outcome you want for this test. Believe it will happen for you. Expect it. Visualize the grade you expect to see and *see* it. Develop a few affirmations or a mantra to help you solidify the intention. Allow your thoughts to remain focused on the desired outcome. Your energy follows your thoughts. Thus, your actions will support this desired outcome.

Remember, this is not about throwing a wish out to the universe and then sitting back and watching TV until test time. If that is your *true* intention, it will become evident in your actions. Because your energy follows your thoughts, you will focus your attention on your intention and study time will inevitably appear and you will be able to use the time more wisely.

Unexpected events:

When a surprise event occurs, and they often do, it is important to quickly step into this process. Take a deep breath and immediately think about the outcome you want and set your intention to achieve it. The universe will respond as quickly as is necessary for your desired outcome. The spiritual realm is not limited by the time and space constraints that we humans have. Do not doubt their abilities. Just set your intention and get busy to achieve it.

If the unexpected event has caused anxiety and/or fear, put the event into proper perspective and empower yourself past it. For example, you are on a run and nearly trample a snake sunning itself on the road. A scream escapes your throat. You immediately take a deep breath and gain a better perspective - thank goodness it wasn't an alligator! I am safe! Take another deep breath and move onward. (I also recommend setting your intention prior to setting off on the run.)

(Make this a part of your lifestyle and you can handle any surprise!)

———— ⸎ ————

Performance Time:

There are several techniques for reducing performance anxiety and fears. When exploring what the anxiety is related to, we often discover it is related to fear of making a mistake, fear of falling, or fear of forgetting lines or choreography. Through this process of making it intentional, we delete the thoughts or comments of doing something out of character (i.e. falling or forgetting), and replace the thought with something better (knowing all the lines, or knowing all the steps in perfect order.)

It is best to literally catch and delete each fear-filled thought as it comes up and replace it with empowering thoughts that support your desired outcome.

When my son was 10 yrs old, he wanted to improve his memory and ability to do ballet combinations in class. He said, "I always forget the combination and then Miss Barbara gets annoyed with me." A self-fulfilling prophecy, right there! I recommended he set his intention prior to the start of each class. We discussed verbiage and he picked what worked best for him. "I am a strong dancer and I remember the combinations easily." From the first day he invoked the intention, he noticed the ease of improvement. So did Miss Barbara.

———— ⸎ ————

Speaking Engagement:

I have heard the most common fear is the fear of public speaking. Now, take a few moments to examine what the real fear is that is coming up for you. It may be associated with the fear of being judged. It could be the fear of making a mistake or fear of what others will think, and so on.

If you walk into the event with the fear of making a mistake, your energy will follow those fearful thoughts and guess what will happen. You will make a mistake just as sure as you said you would. Delete the fearful thoughts as they come up and replace them with empowering thoughts more aligned with the outcome you desire.

Most likely, you desire to have ease of flow with your verbiage and positive reception from the guests. Set your intention and allow your thoughts to focus on what you want to happen. Your energy will follow your thoughts and you will practice with ease. When an anxious thought arises, cancel it and replace it.

Event/Party Planning:

Determine the purpose of the event you are planning. Set your intention for the desired outcome. It may be as simple as the guest of honor appreciating the event. Or it may be as complex as seeing clear and appropriate weather for an outside wedding and reception. Regardless, set your intention. Believe it will be so. Expect your desired outcome and nothing less.

When doubts creep into your thoughts, delete them and replace them with positive thoughts about the desired outcome. If others are involved, make sure they are on board with you. Otherwise you may find yourself waving away their comments as you cancel and delete the pessimistic energies they bring to the planning.

Gift Giving:

Always examine and know your intention in giving gifts. No matter how simple the gift may be, there is always an intention behind the giving.

If your intention is altruistic or benevolent in nature and you are not seeking some sort of return, then give and enjoy the giving. However, if your intention is less than honorable, has a thread of selfishness within it or some sort of hidden agenda, reconsider the giving of the gift.

For those who give a gift because it is the "right thing to do" or because "they gave me one so I have to reciprocate", your intention deserves more reflection and contemplation. Are you lovingly bringing balance to the situation? Would you be giving this gift if you hadn't received one from them? Do you begrudge the act of reciprocating the gift giving?

Once you have determined the purpose for giving the gift and examined your true intention behind the giving, then you can focus on the desired outcome for the recipient and set your intention for how it will be received. Intending that the receiver enjoys and appreciates the gift is enough.

Gift giving from obligation means it comes with an expectation of some deeper meaning which deserves further exploration.

Job Interview:

While considering the intention for seeking this job, also visualize having the job and notice what you feel. Does it feel wonderful and in alignment with who you are and what you want for this life?

Maybe it does not feel in alignment but you are going to attend the interview anyway. Set your intention for the interview. An intention that the interviewer will clearly see the value in your abilities is appropriate. It's always good to have the intention that you speak easily, effortlessly, and clearly.

I always recommend adding a layer to the intention like this: "If this position is for my best potential and highest good, allow my talents and skills to align well with the position and allow the interviewer to see it clearly." If the position is not in your best interest at this time, the universe will allow for a good interview and you will feel good about it. However, the position will go to someone who is more aligned with it at this time. Some people call that "A God thing." I call it Divine Intervention!

Making a Major Purchase:

When making a major purchase, we often narrow the hunt down to the final two or three choices we like best. We like this one for these reasons and we like the other for those reasons. It can be an ordeal to determine which one will finally be ours.

I recommend setting your intention prior to beginning the actual hunt. Set your intention for the best possible item for you at this time. Then let the universe conspire to bring you the best one. Be open to what comes forward. It may not be what you would have initially picked. But when we set our intention for the best possible outcome and we expect it, then we accept it into our reality, and thus it will be!

Final Notes

We can push, bully, force, or bulldoze our way through a situation to make a desired outcome materialize. However, if we have to push it through and force it to happen that means it is being met with resistance. The resistance is our sign it may not be in alignment with our life path or purpose.

Because we have free will, we can co-create with the universe in any direction we choose. The best outcomes are those we allow to come together with our intention focused on what is best for us or is in close alignment with our greatest potential and life purpose.

When we pay attention to our intention, we see things we didn't see before and we understand *more!*

Empowerment Prayer

God Empower me with the ability to
Seek positive perspectives in all I do
Speak my truth with clarity and respect
and to Share empowering wisdom with Grace

Barbette Spitler 2015

My wish for you...

*that you will harness the power
of positive perspectives and
embrace the freedom that comes when
allowing the past to be healed.*

Appendix

Disempowering Thoughts/Statements

I can't_____

I don't understand

No one understands me

I never _____

I am depressed

I always get sick

I'm not smart enough

I always do things backwards

No one cares

My Guardian Angel is on vacation

Things are too hard

I'm overwhelmed

No one listens

WE have the worst luck

I never win anything

_____ happens every time

_____ has NO common sense

I struggle in school

I'm losing my memory

I have the memory of a gnat

I forget everything

I can't find anything

I always lose my _____

Every time _____ this happens

I have a fear of_____

I hate _____

Again?

We have the worst luck

I shouldn't

I can't forgive

I have _____(cancer, disease)

My _____ (illness, injury, disease)

I hate getting old.

Empowering Thoughts/Affirmations

I can_____

I will_____

_____ is easy for me

I AM smart enough, good

enough... enough

I belong

I am safe

I am surrounded by people who care

My family loves and respects me

I am comfortable with _____

WE have the best luck

We do well always

I am optimistic it will happen

I respect myself and others

I remember and recall easily

My memory is efficient

I am delightful

I bring happiness with me

I am surrounded by joy

We get the best service

I forgive with grace

I am well respected

I am surrounded with love

I give love easily and freely

We are always safe and protected

I work with great people

I enjoy my job

I enjoy my life

I am happy

I am organized

My body heals itself quickly and easily

I am a good and loving person

I can find everything I need

I like who I am

Every day I'm getting better and better

Glossary of Barbette-ism's

Delete and Re-think It – The process of clearing the energy of disempowering thoughts and choosing a better option more aligned with the desired outcome. Used in conjunction with emotion (with or without animated gestures) is a very powerful process. It requires pondering.

Do-Over's – Similar to Delete and Re-think It. When we have a disempowering thought, we catch it – release it and take the opportunity to think an empowering thought instead. Just because it is "out there" doesn't mean we are stuck with it – we can think it differently. We do-it-over-again.

Intention Means Everything – It just does! When you pay attention to your intention you see what you didn't see before and you understand more.

Limiting Belief – A belief we hold, regardless of its truth, that limits us. It could be a simple, single layer belief or complex, multi-layered belief. Both are limiting our forward momentum on the journey toward a desired outcome.

Pinball Machine of Life – Life without purposeful intention is life as the silver ball in a pinball machine. It means being bumped around and whacked often by anything else in the universal flow. It doesn't feel good. It isn't healthy. More importantly, it is painful.

Ripple Roadblock – Someone or something that stops the flow of energy of the Ripple Effect. It could be a blessing to block the flow of negativity rippling from an unpleasant event. It could be someone soaking up the flow of positivity and immersing in it rather than allowing it to affect them and then share that positivity with others.

Stinkin' Thinkin' – Disempowered thinking for self or others. This type of thinking is low vibrational frequency. It includes pessimistic or judgmental thoughts of self or others.

Spitler's Law – The magnificent mayhem we created for ourselves where everything that could go wrong did. We believed it was ten times worse than Murphy's Law. And, for us it was!

Triple P Approach – The pathway to finding a purposeful, positive perspective. It requires proactive thought and action to achieve the expected result.

Word Vomit – What some people call "venting" I call word vomit. You literally throw up all the verbiage and emotional connection to it. Because it is laced with negativity, it must be cleaned up quickly.

About the Author

Barbette was raised on a small farm near Dayton, Ohio. She has always had a special connection with animals of all kinds and sizes. Although she didn't understand it as a child, she was able to communicate with them on an energetic level. Her level of empathy was, at times, distressing to her. She knew when the animals were well or ill. She understood the animal kingdom and had a strong desire to work with them. She fancied herself to be the next Dr. Dolittle. But, Barbette also had the same empathic abilities with people. That, too, was confusing and often distressing for her as a child. Her desire to help people became so strong though, she decided to become a nurse.

In the early years of Barbette's twenty-five year nursing career, her focus on health and well-being was ignited. She became aware that the absence of disease does not necessarily mean good health. She became determined to help others by promoting health and wellness and teaching ways to prevent disease. Barbette sought out holistic modalities and soon became proficient in each of them. She has achieved numerous certifications in a variety of programs. She became a Specialist in Energy Medicine, and an instructor for several energy medicine modalities including: Quantum Touch™, and TYLEM through Energy Medicine Partnerships. She is the founder of Angel Medicine™, A Transformational Certification Program. She is proficient in her work for both humans and animals.

Barbette is currently working on a Master's to PhD. program in Complementary and Alternative Medicine.

She continues to work with and teach positive perspectives. She offers up a positive perspective at every given opportunity. Frequently, the viewpoint offered is just what the receiver needed to resolve a situation or heal an incident. Those moments are life-altering, life-changing and life-improving. These are empowering moments which allow us to be free of the emotional drains of woundedness and hurt. And with each step we are creating a ripple effect of positivity which resonates without end. As we learn and understand how the ripple effect of our self empowerment improves the lives of those around us, we are more likely to be proactive in our self care. Thus begins the process of harnessing positive perspectives and making it intentional!

Notes

Notes

Notes

Notes

Notes

Notes

Notes

Notes

Notes

Notes